Dieses Malbuch gehört:

....

Ich bin ..... Jahre alt.

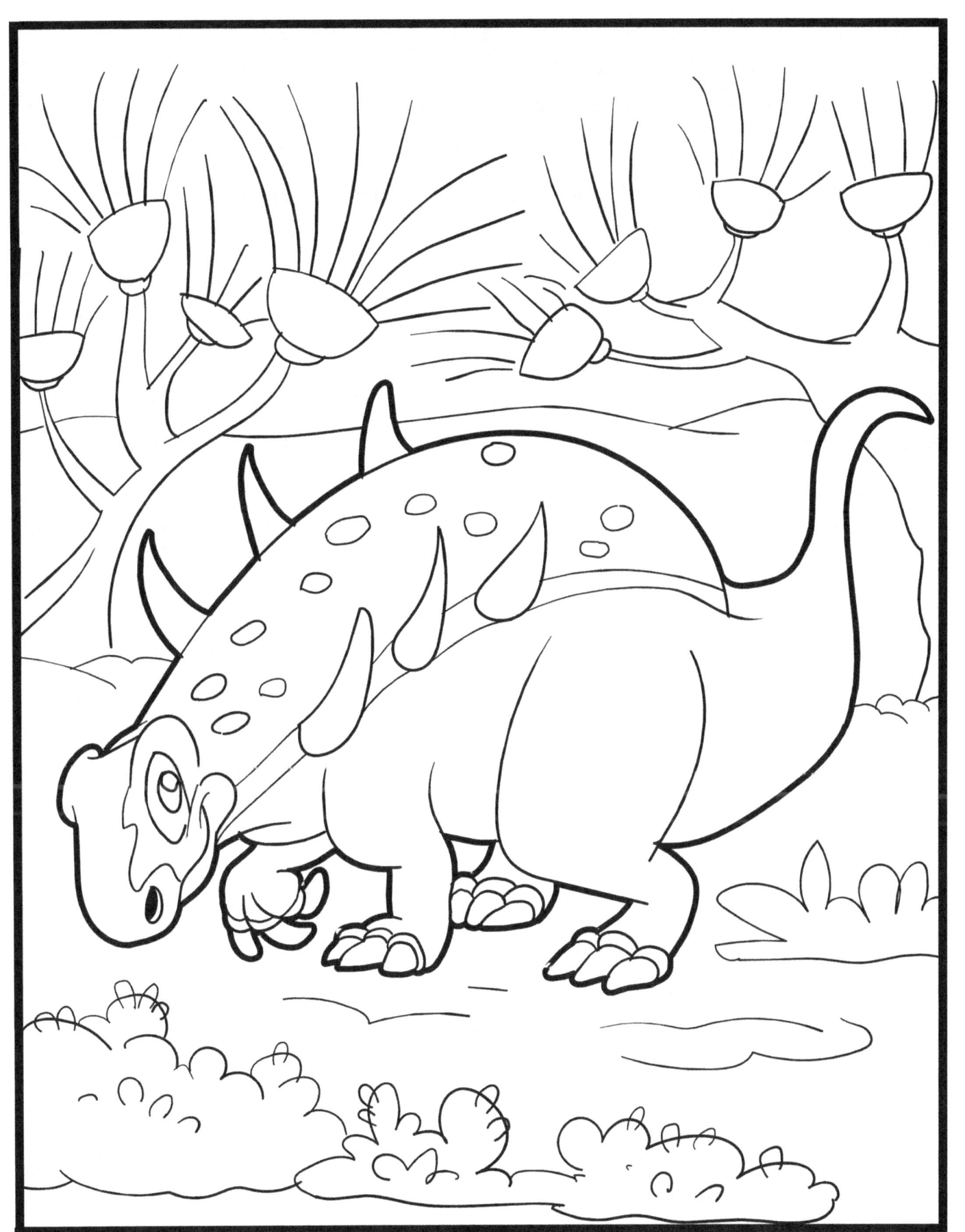

Akanthopholis

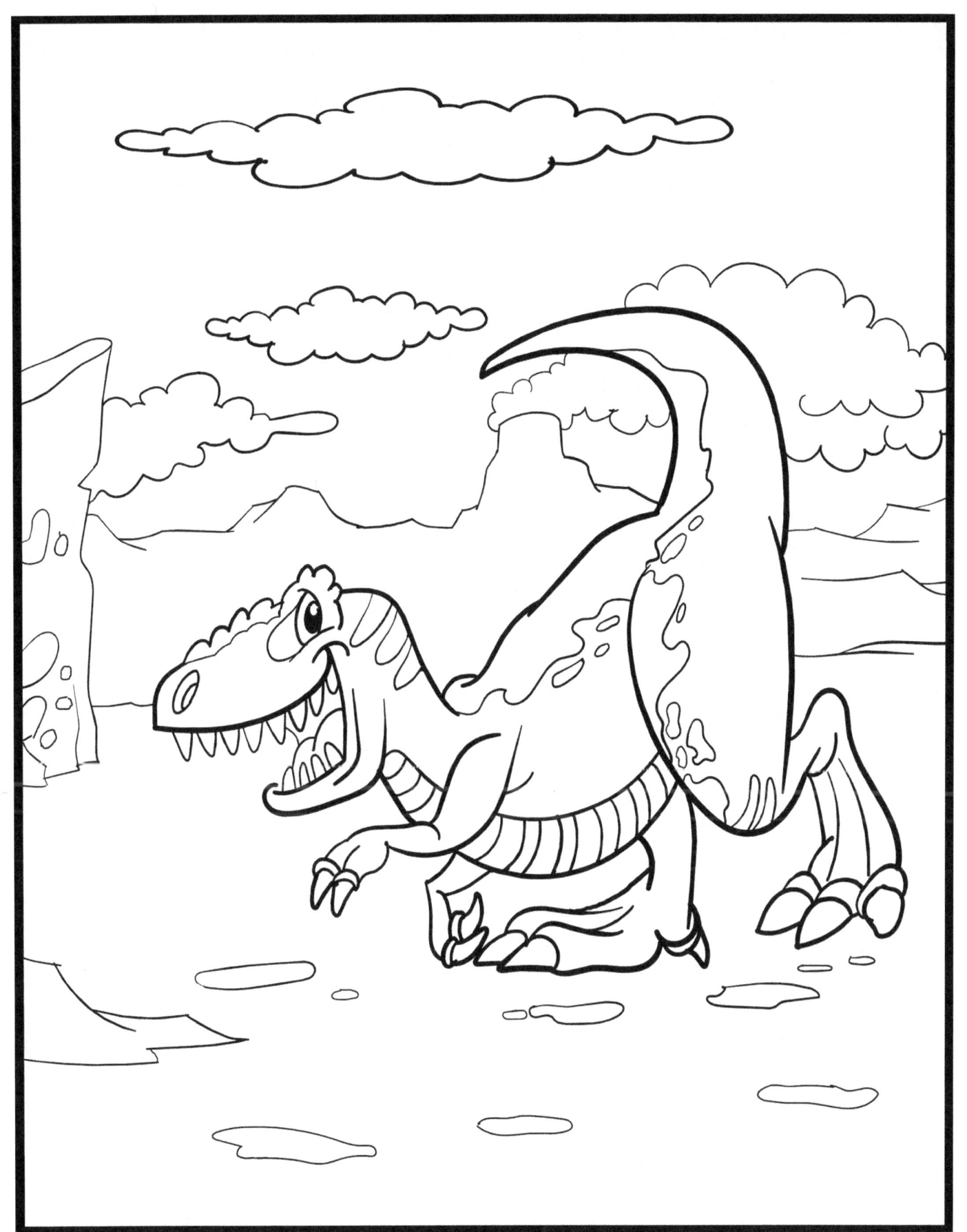

Allosaurus

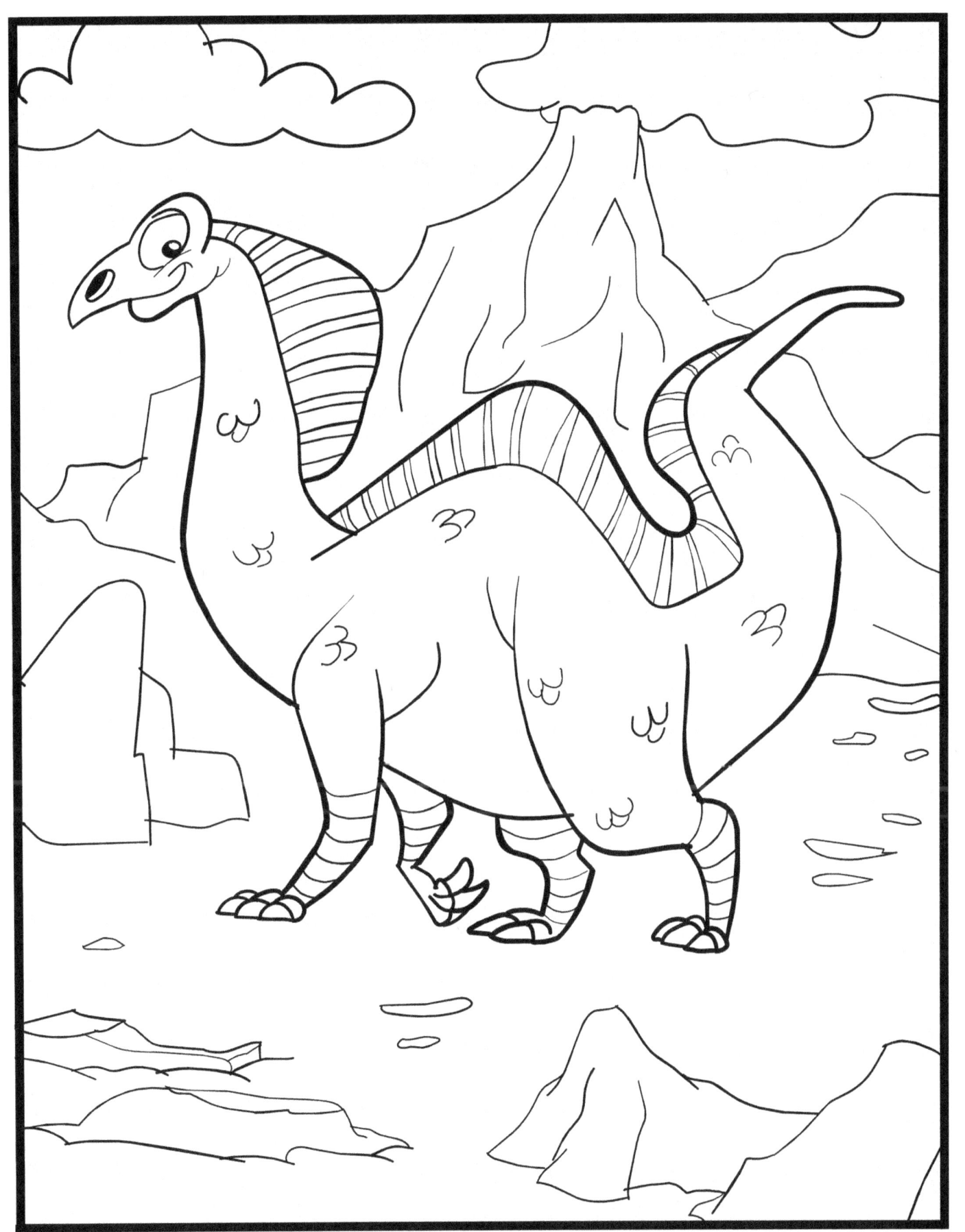

Amargasurus

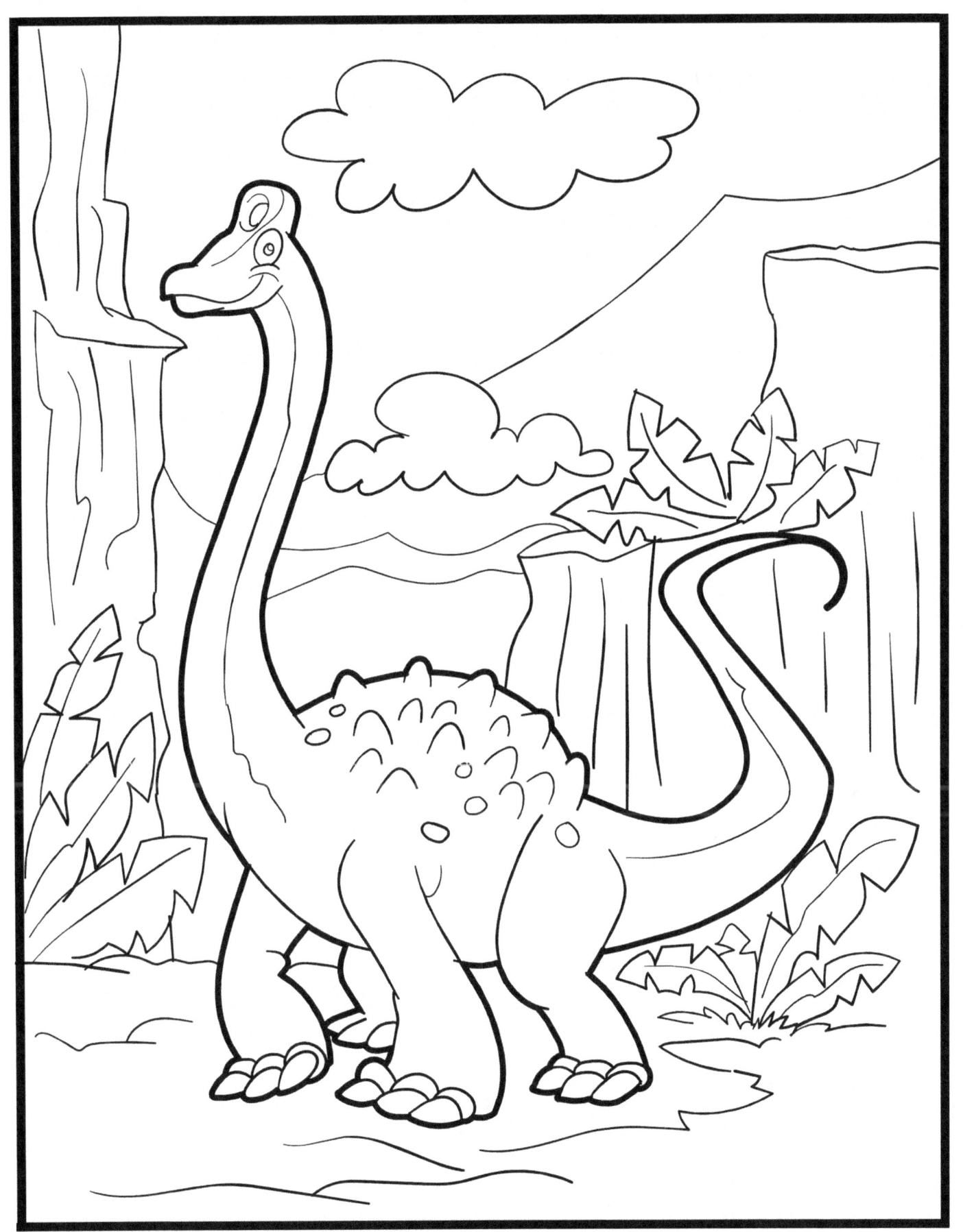

Andesaurus

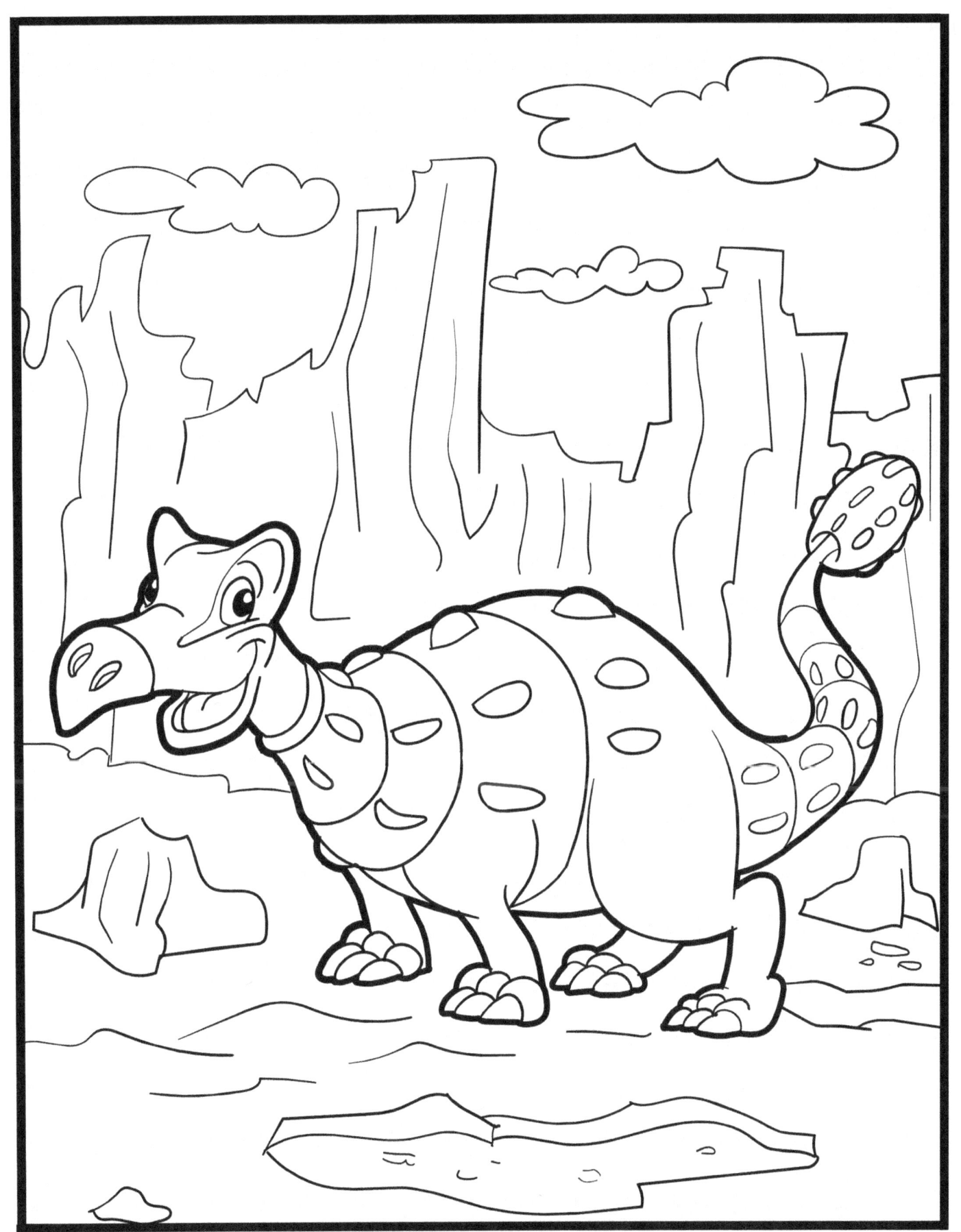

Ankilosaurus

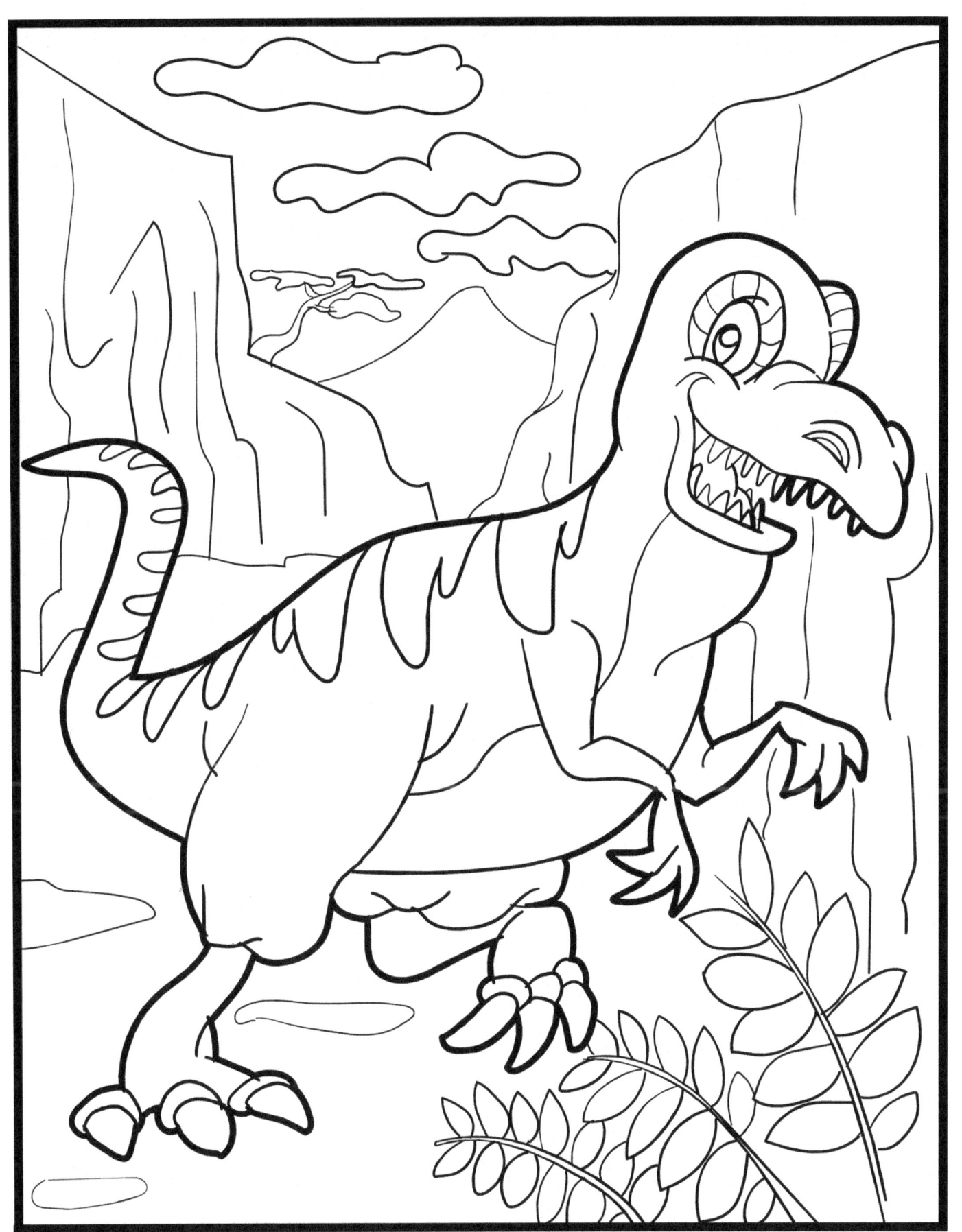

Baryonyx

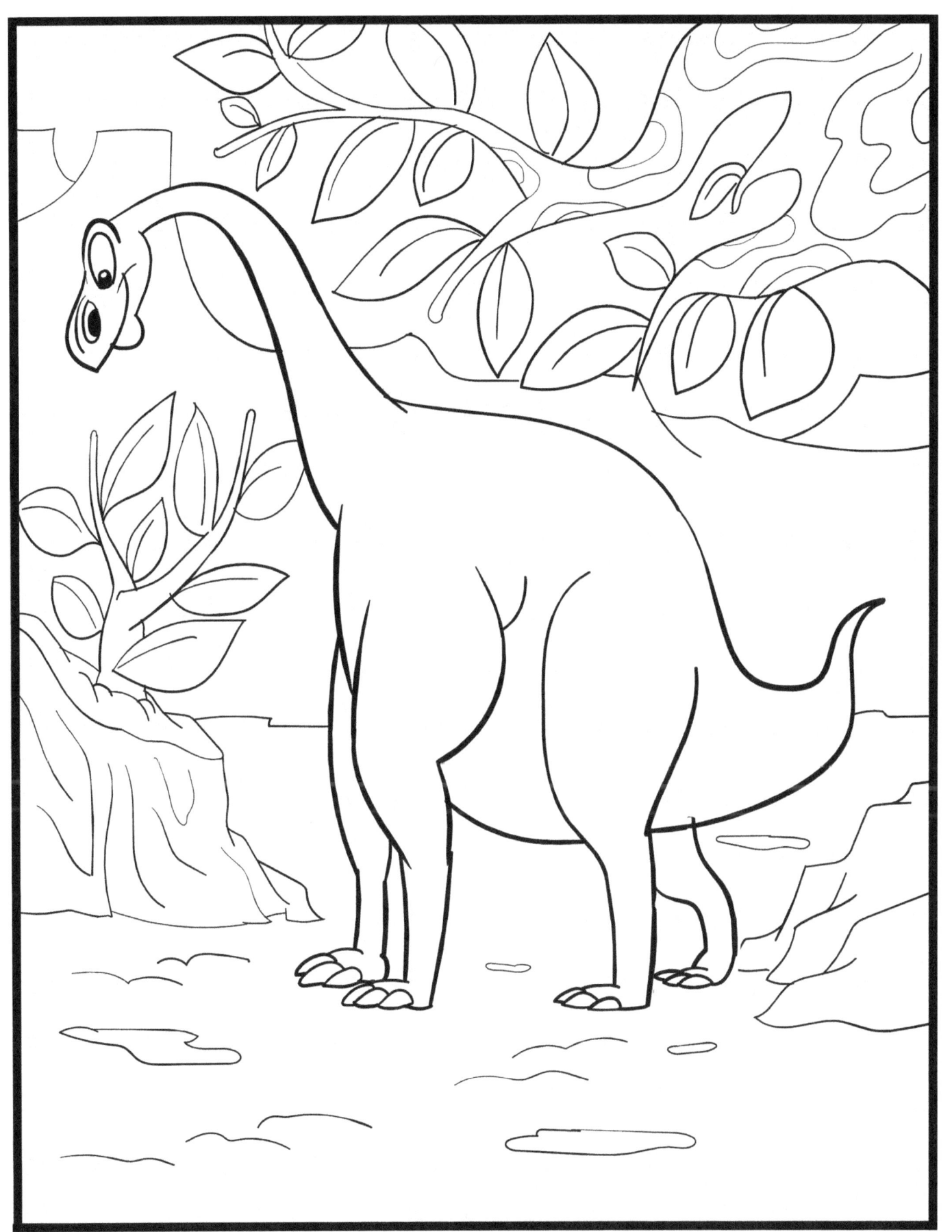

Brachiosaurus

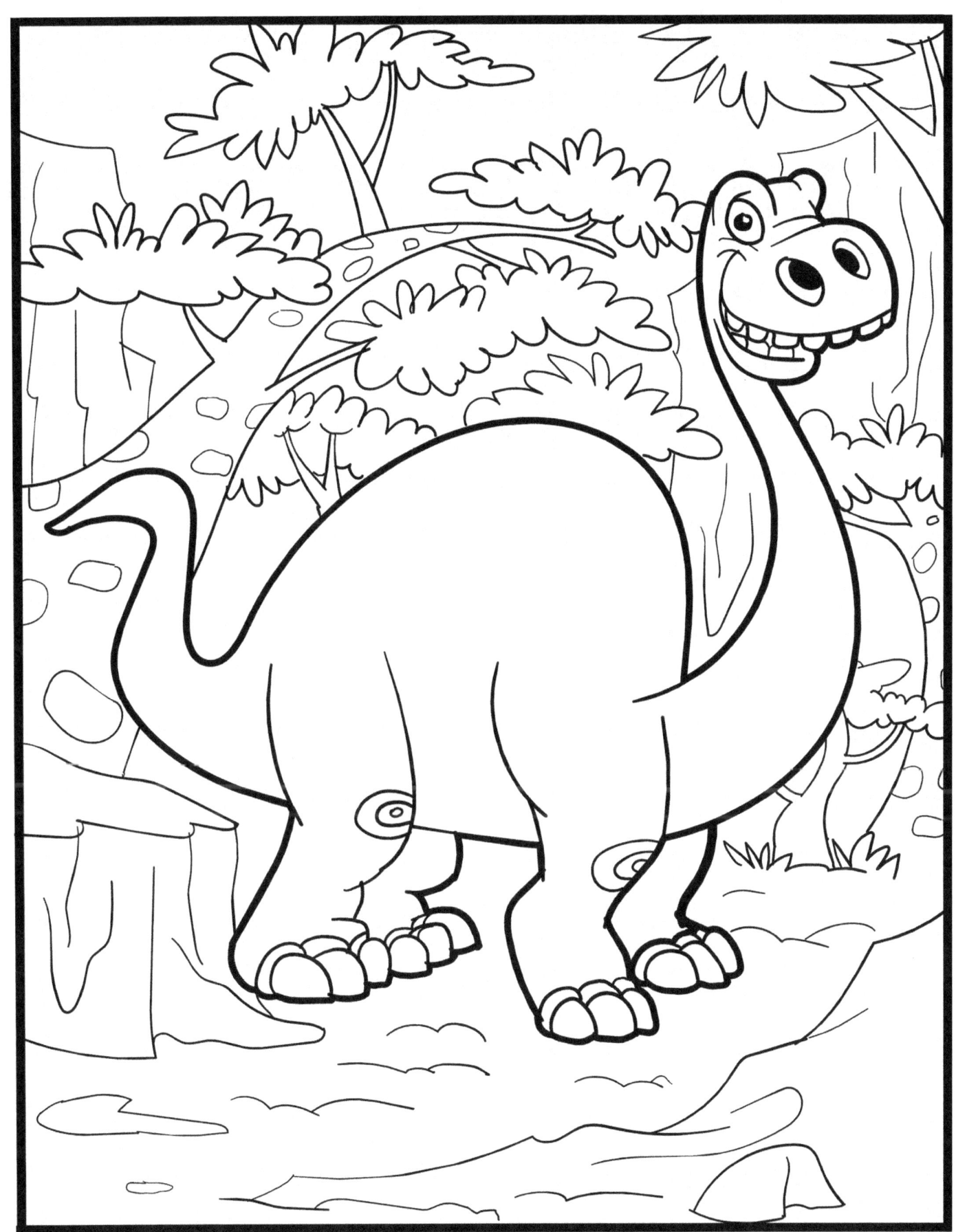

Brontosaurus

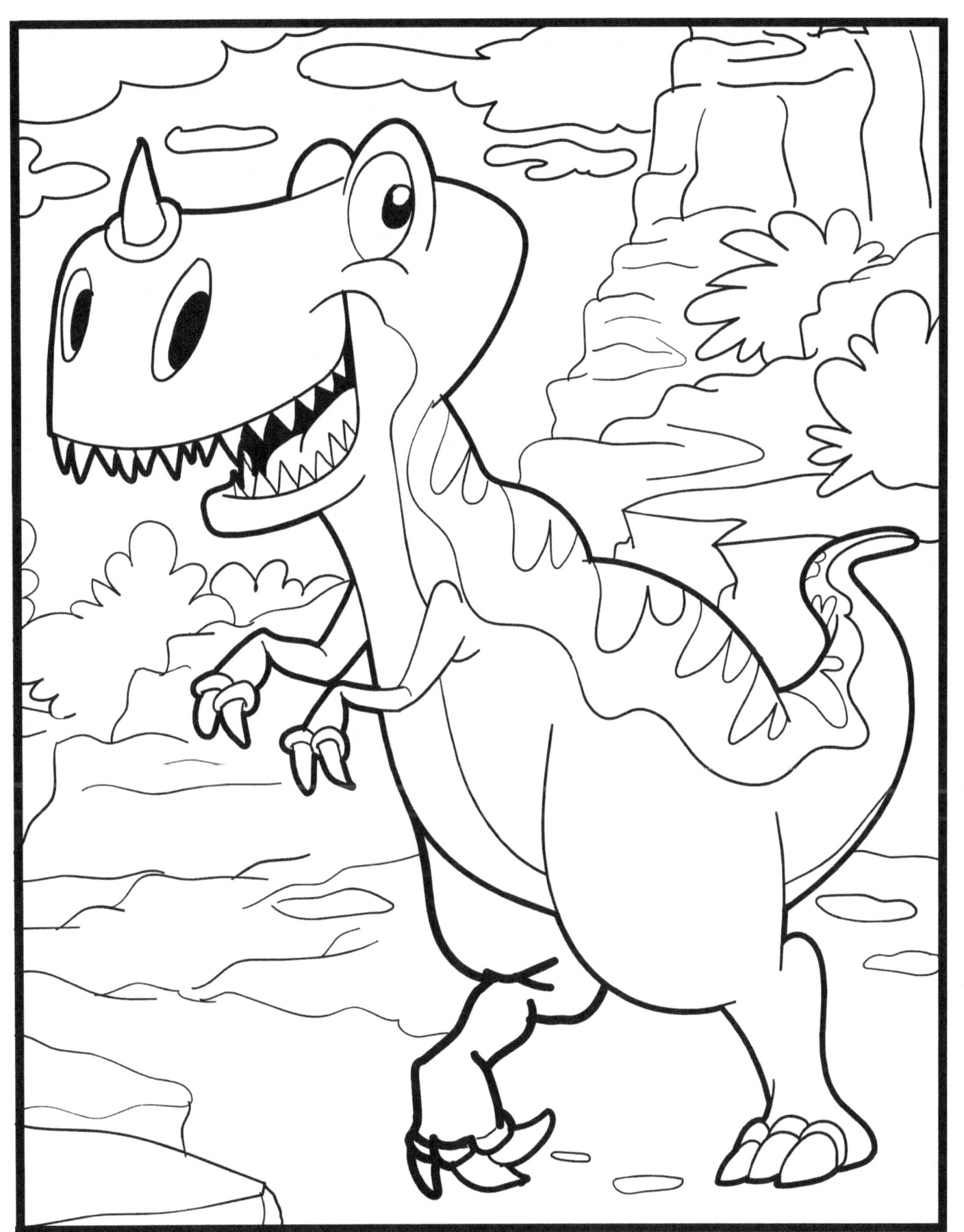

Carnosaurus

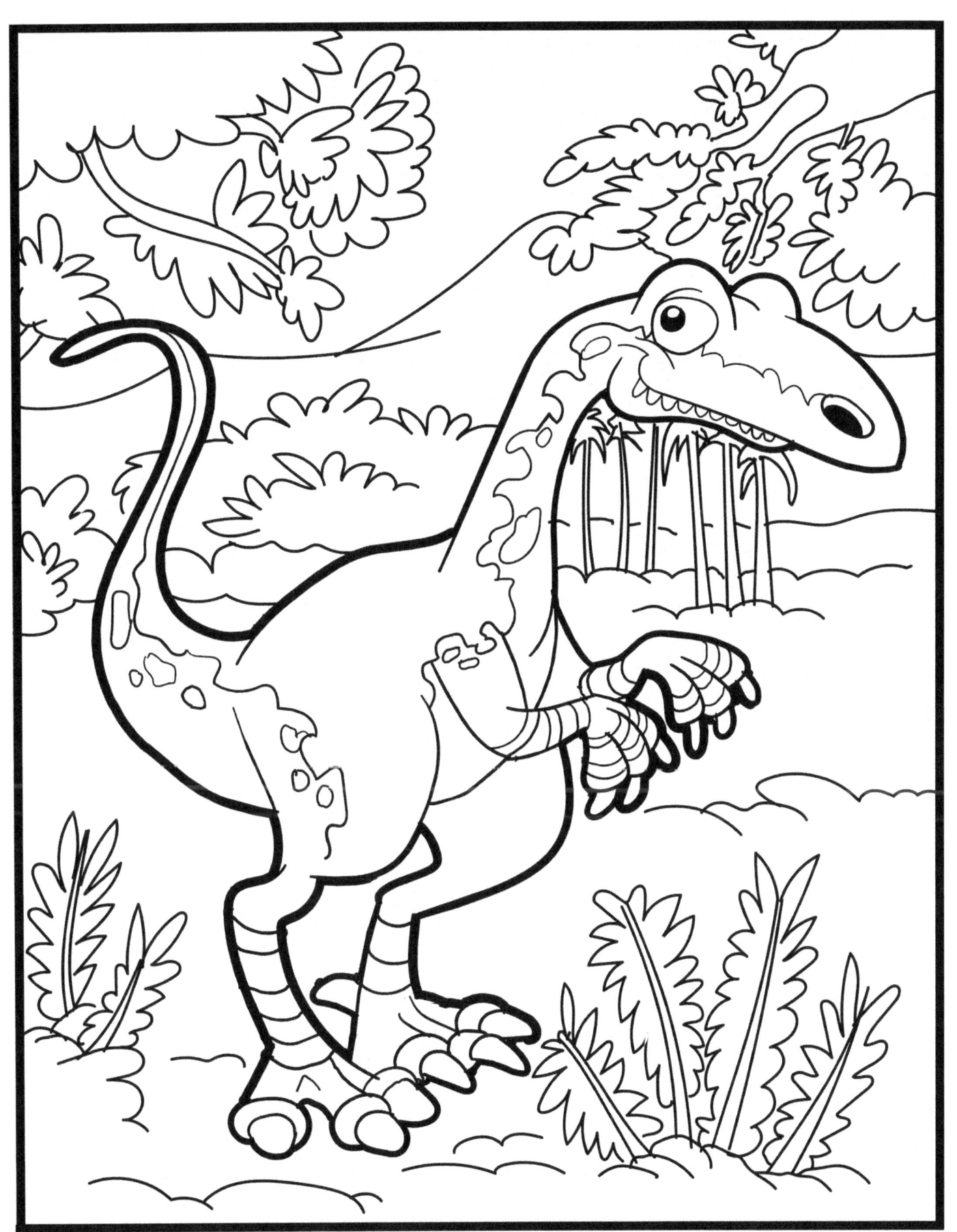

Coelophysis

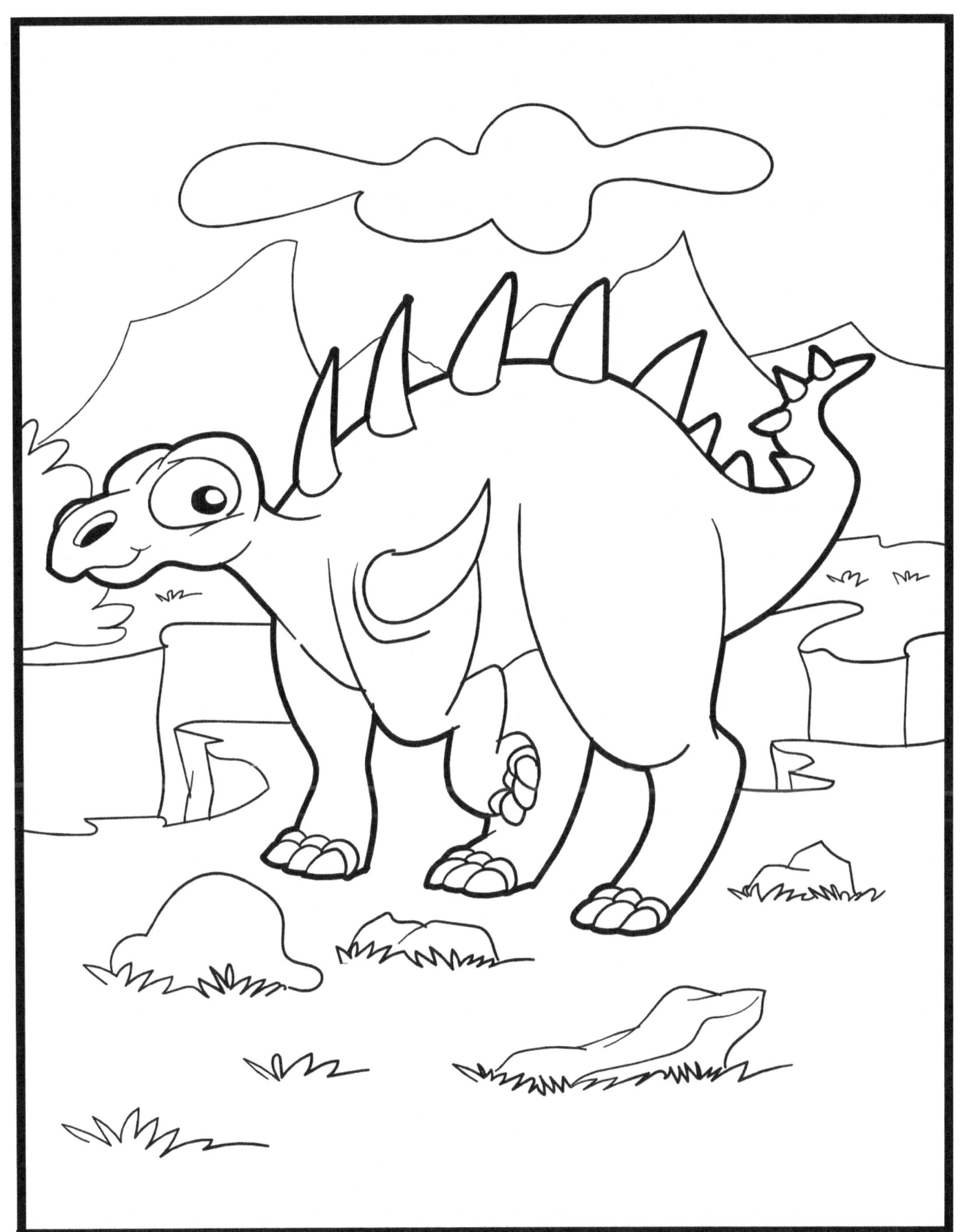

Dacentrurus

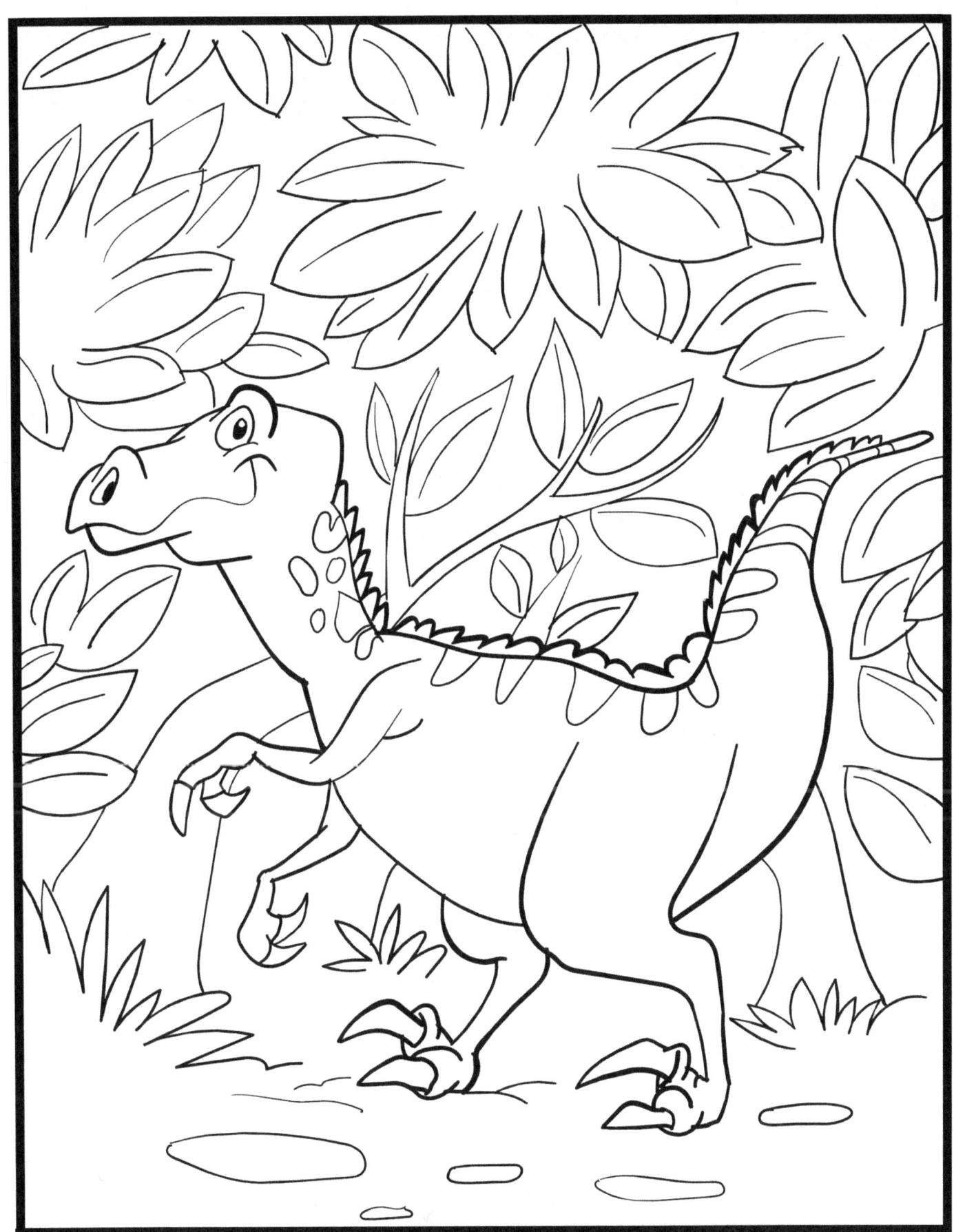

Deinonychus

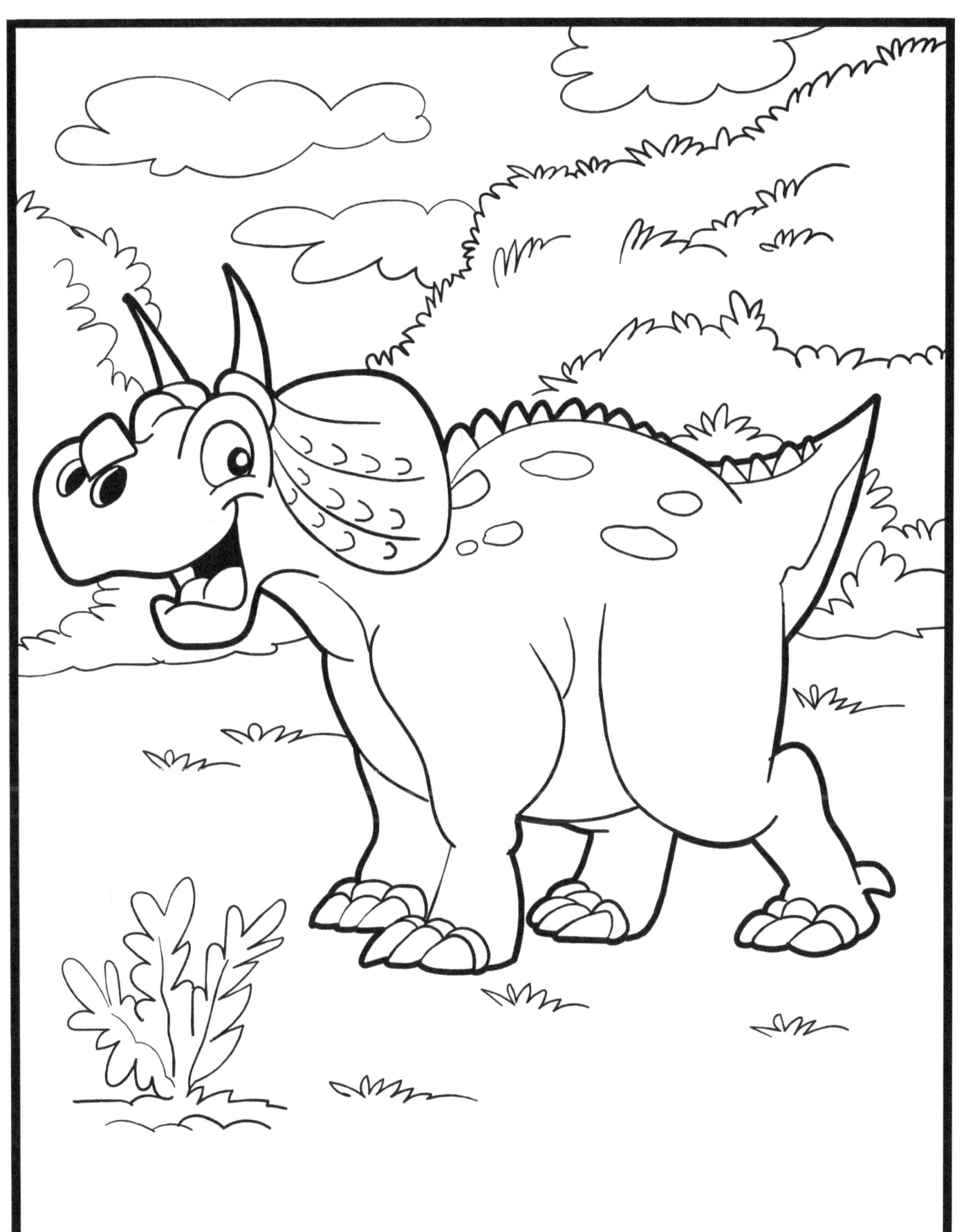

Diceraptor

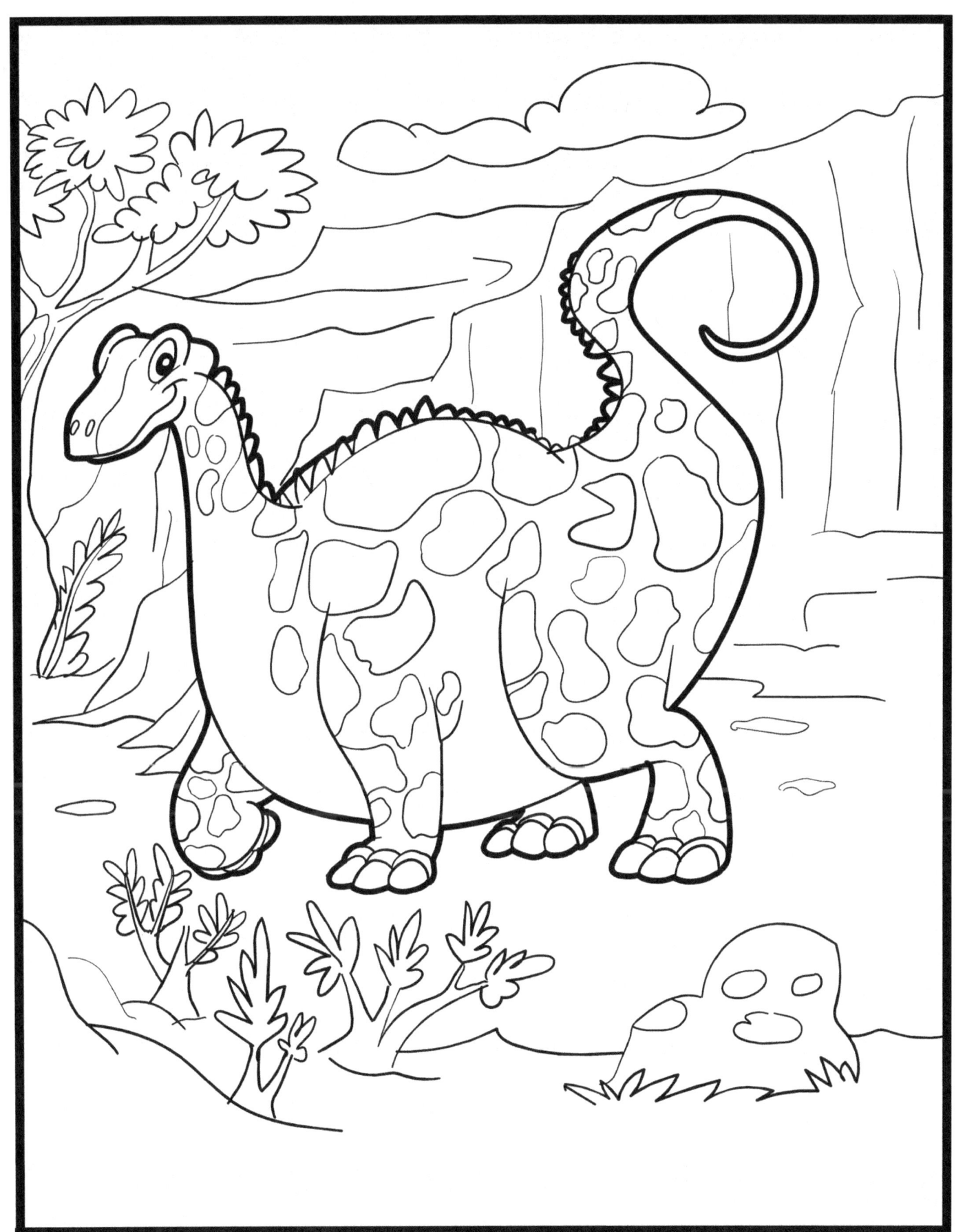

Dicraeosaurus

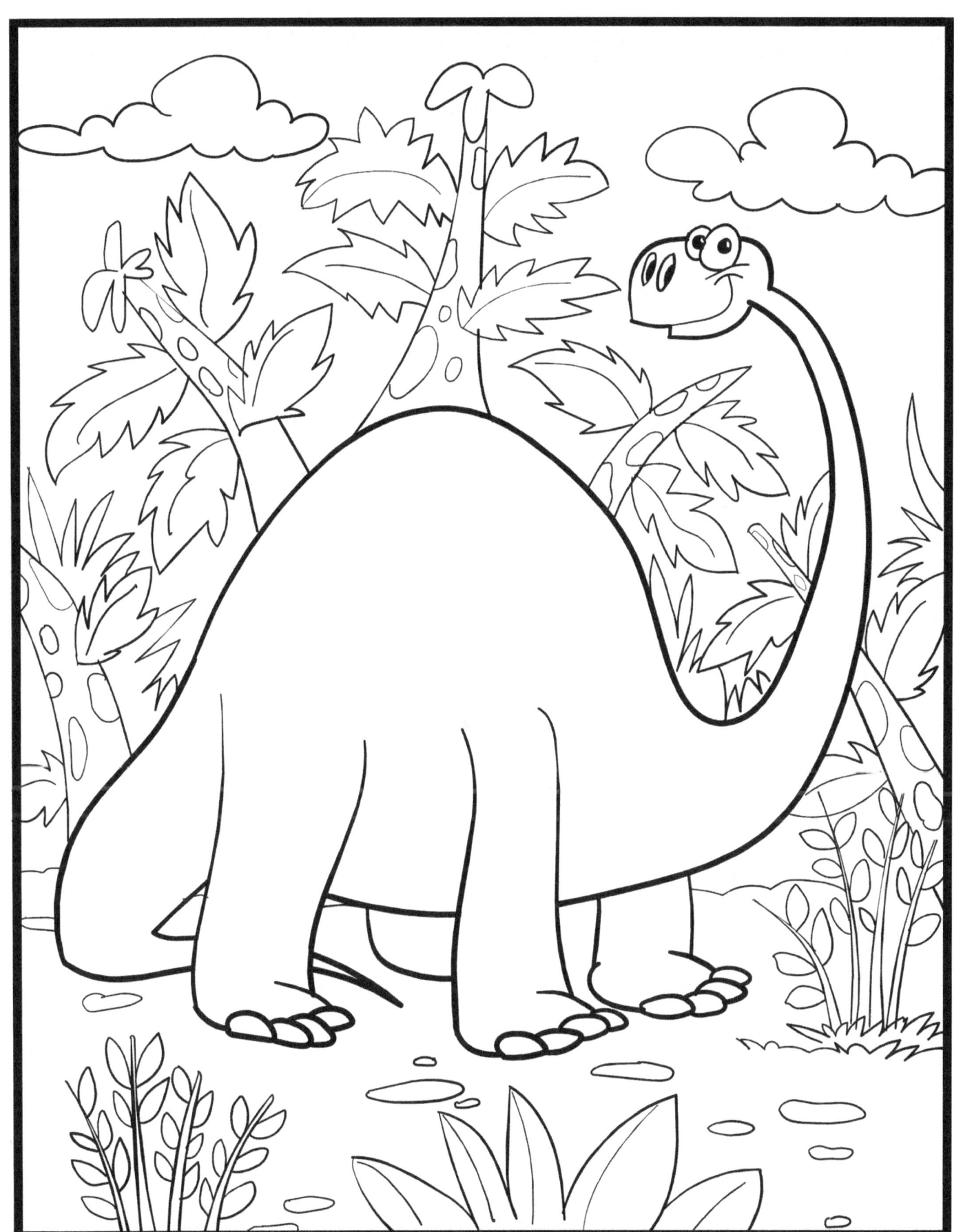

Diplodocus

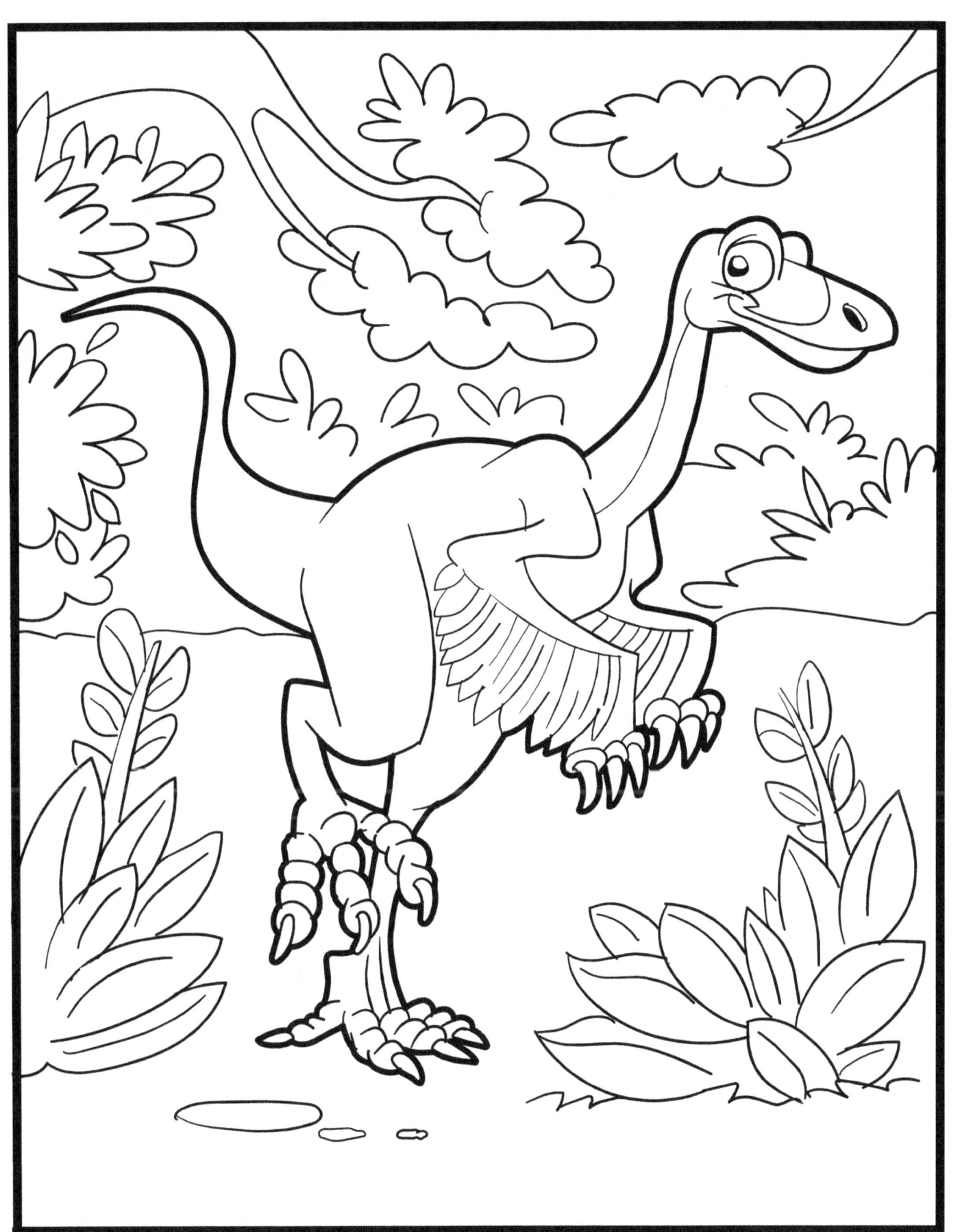

Dromaeosaurus

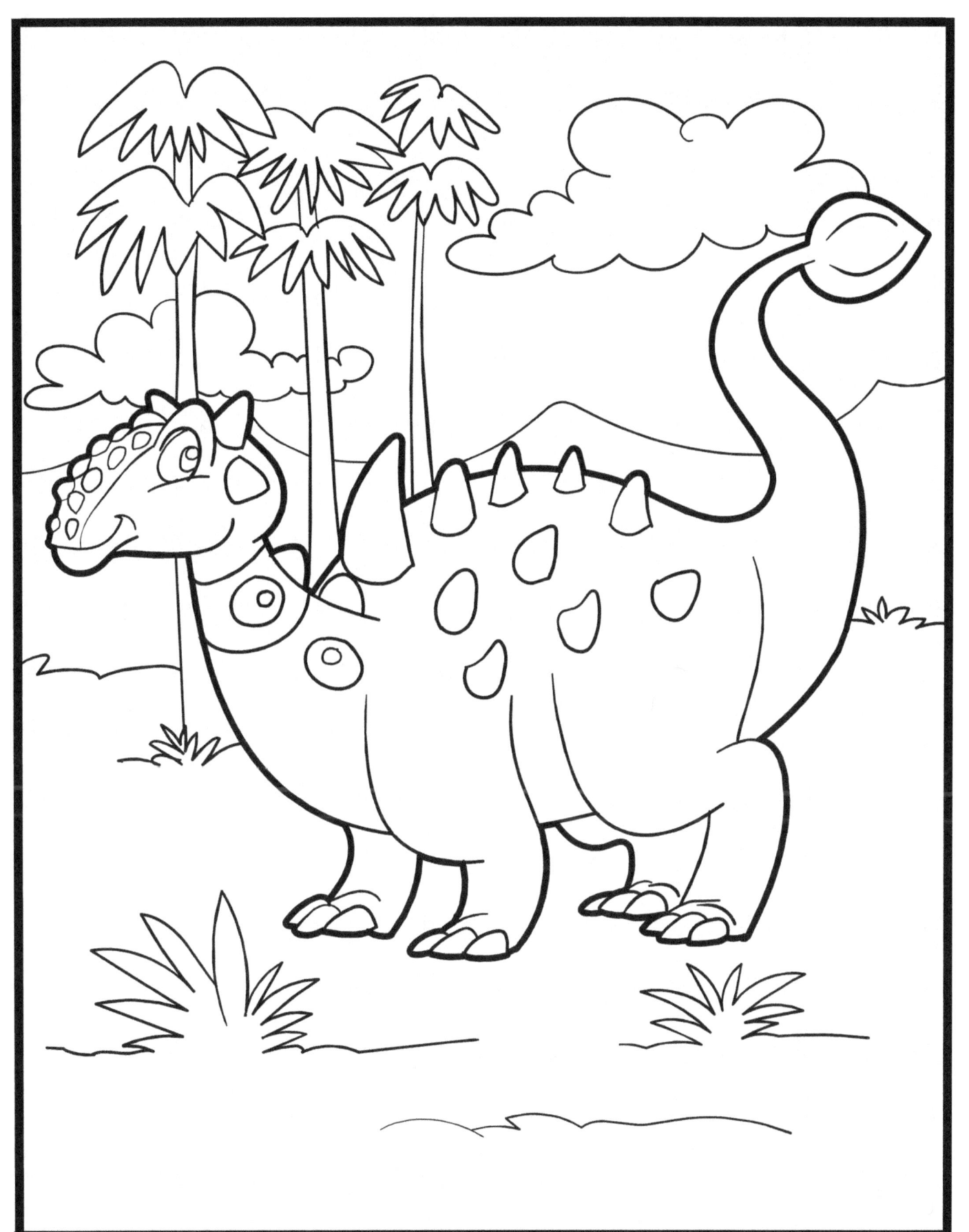

Euoplocephalus

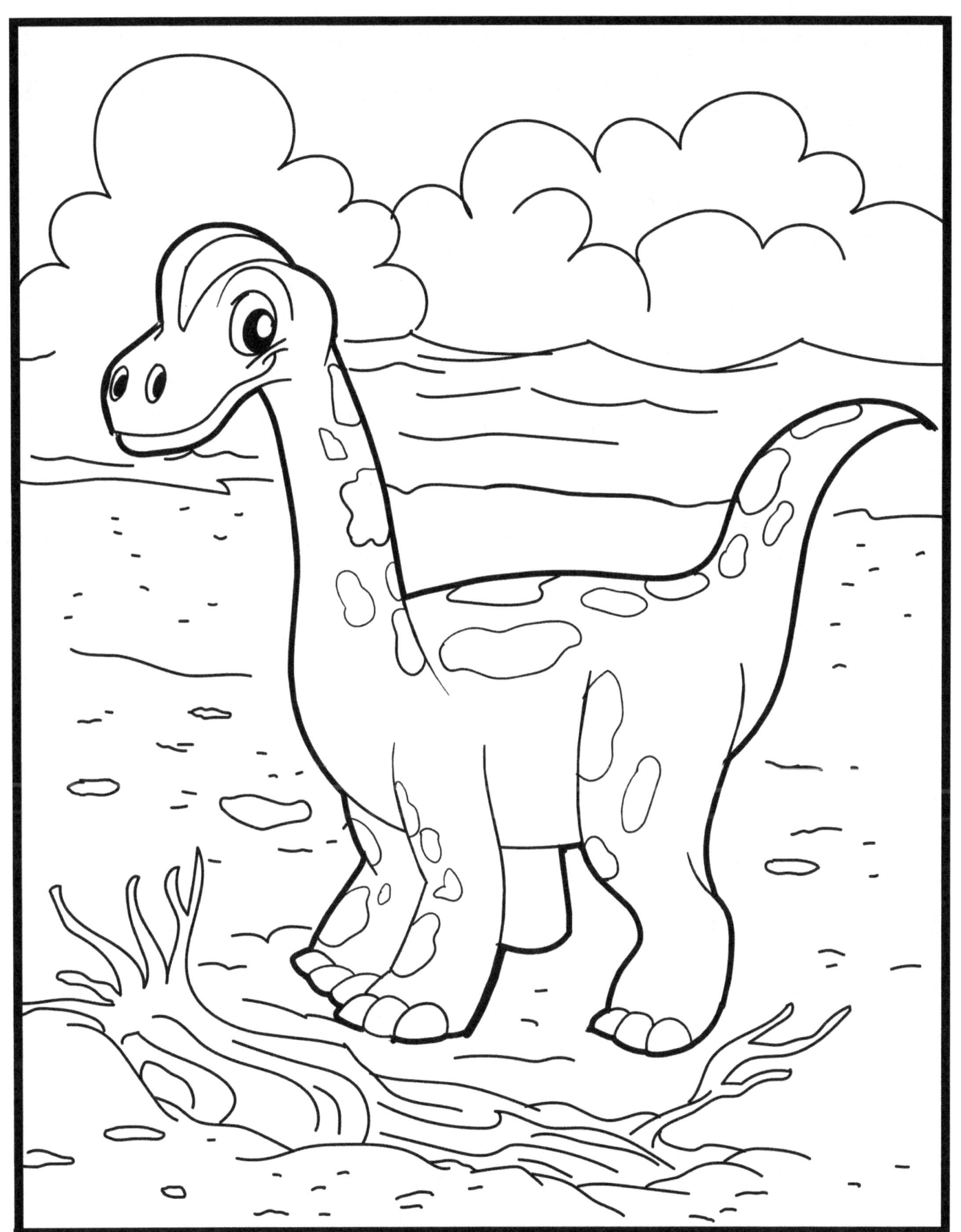

Europasaurus

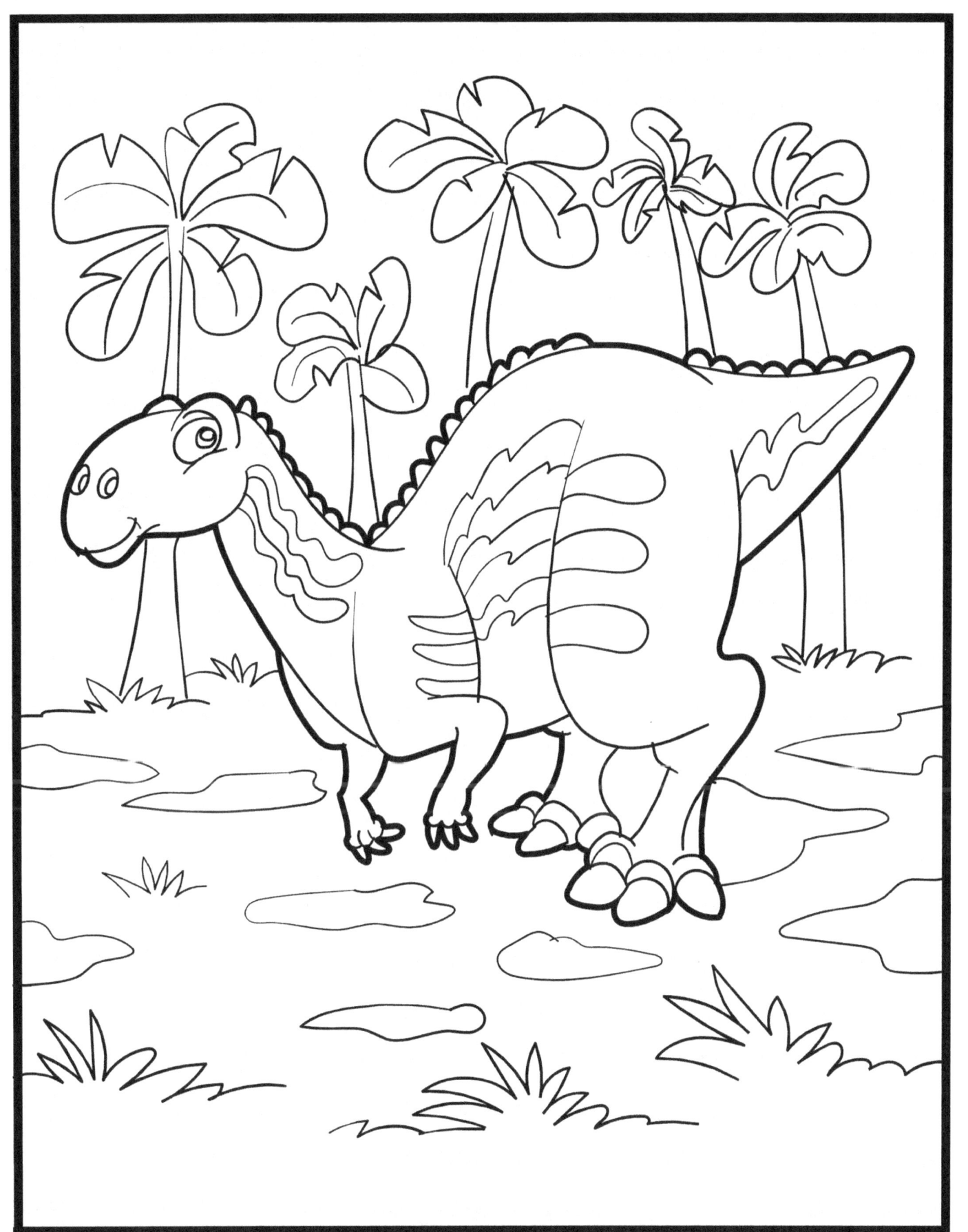

Fukuisaurus

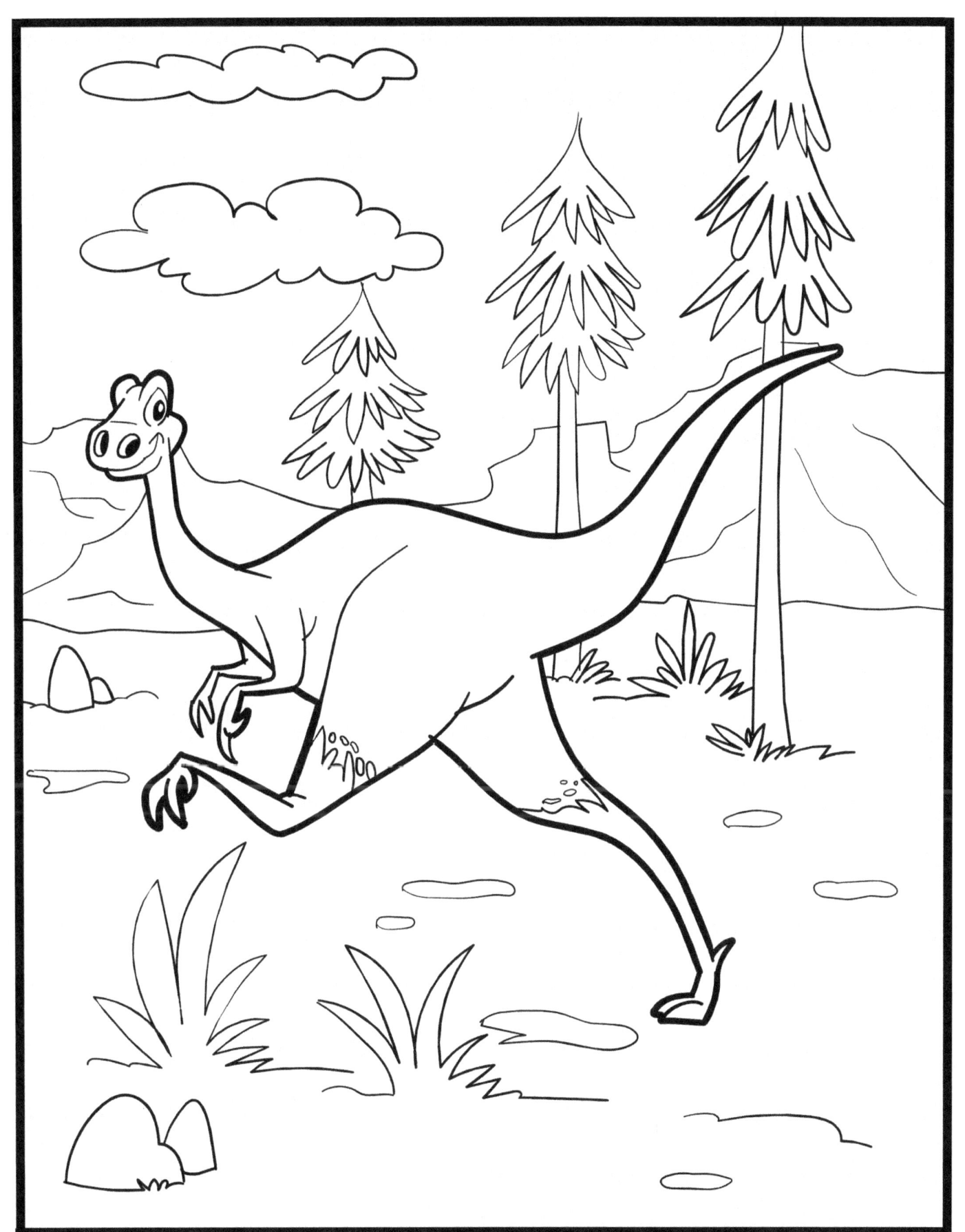

Gallimino

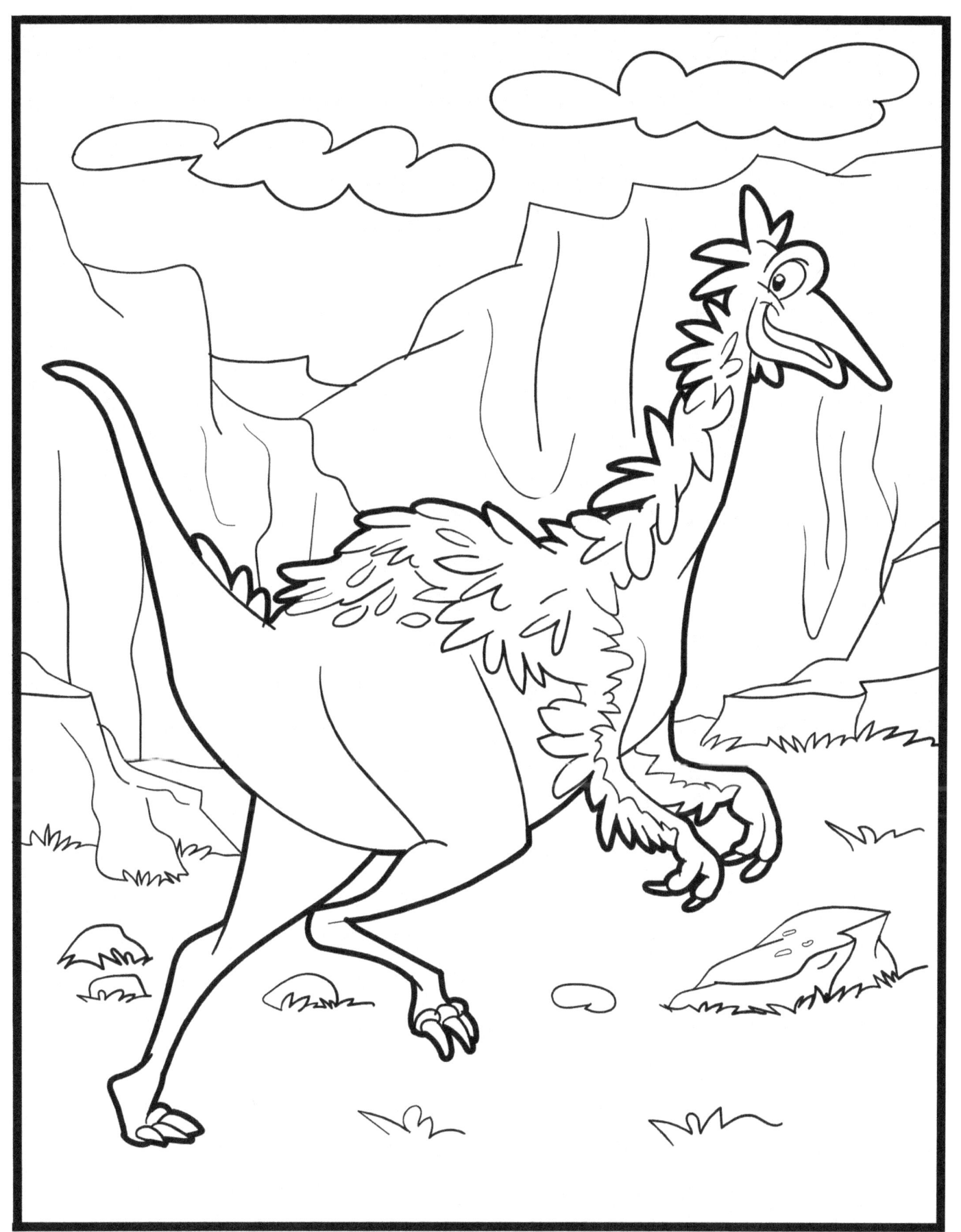

Garudimimus

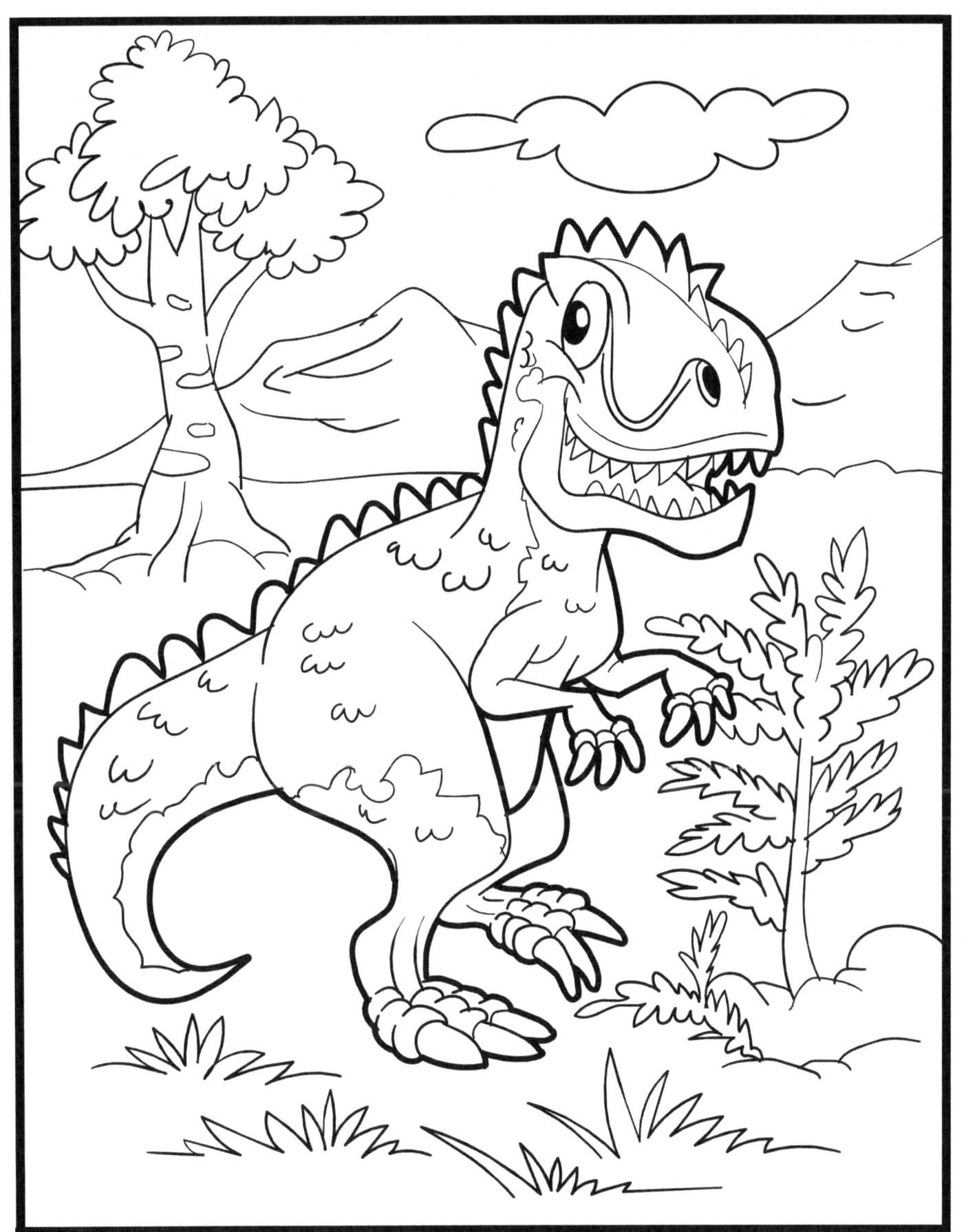

Gigantosaurus

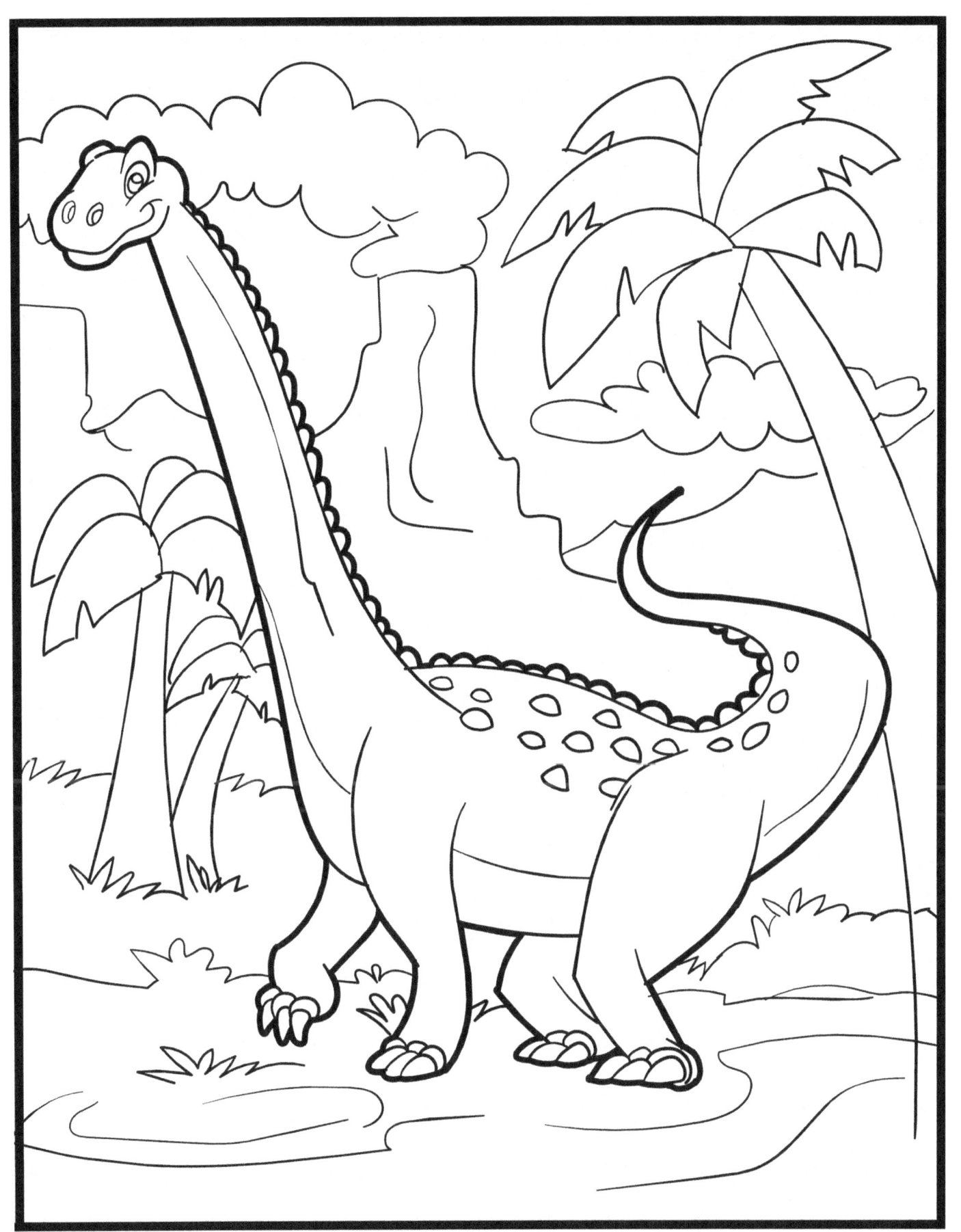

Hanenschia

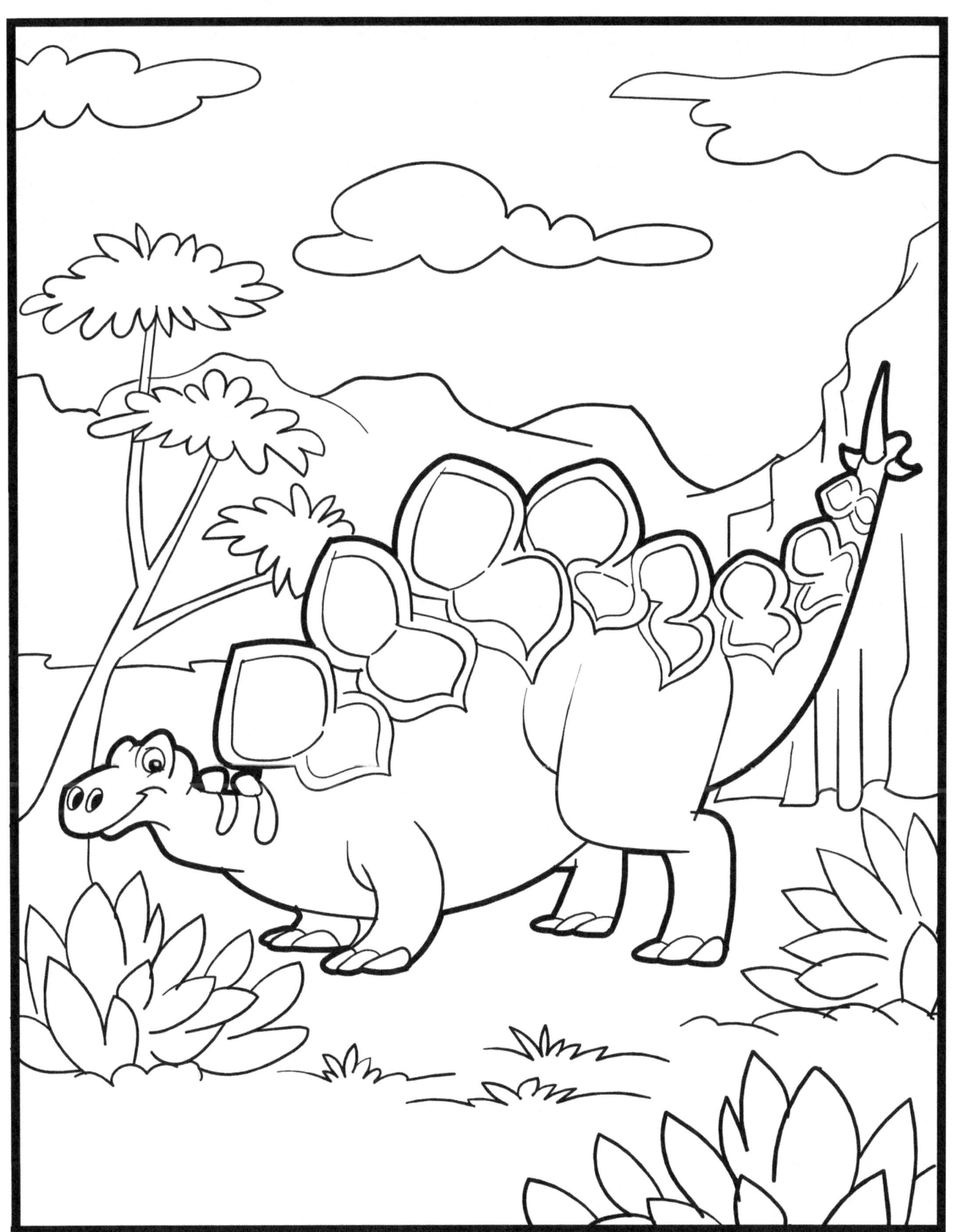

Hesperosaurus

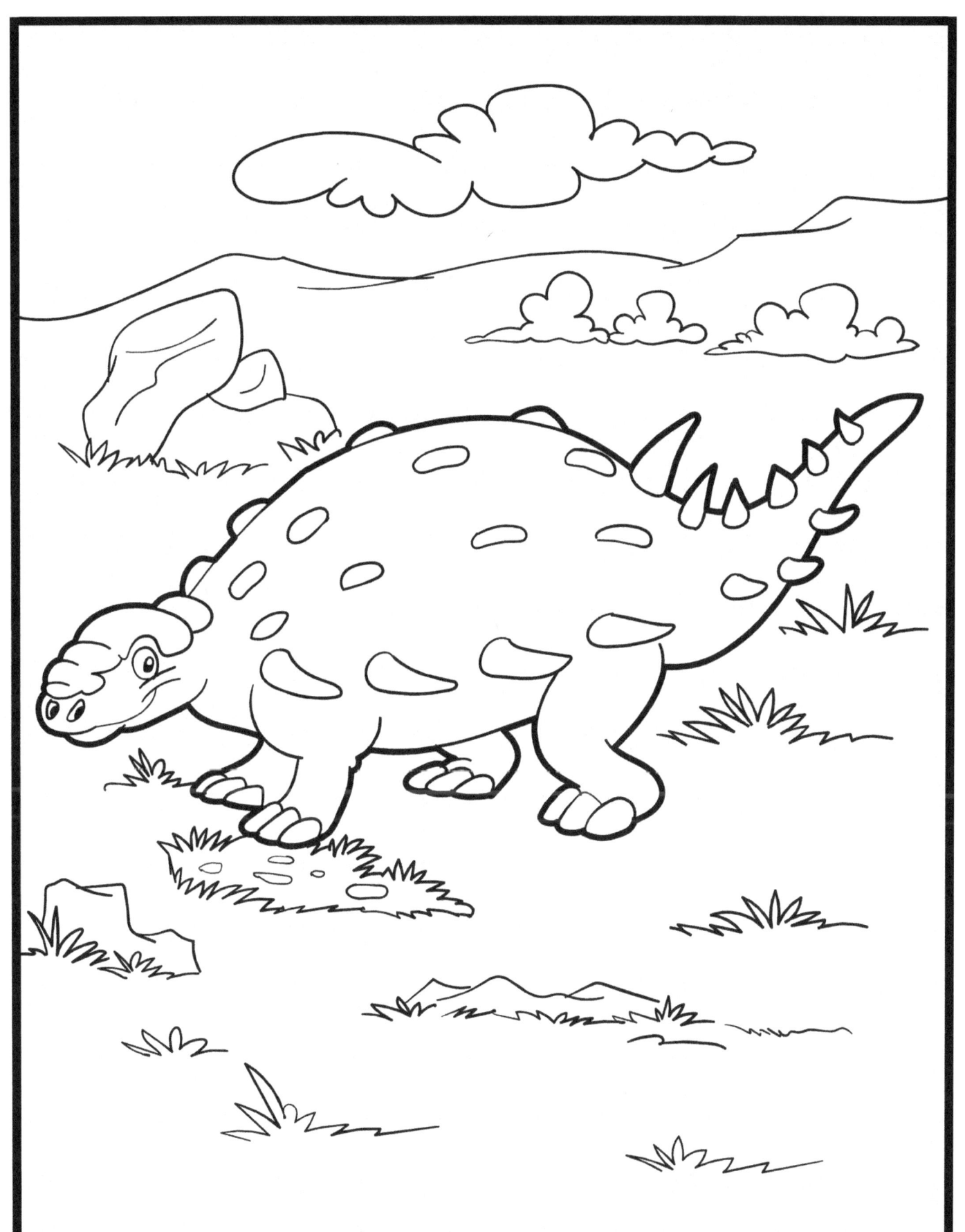

Hylaeosaurus

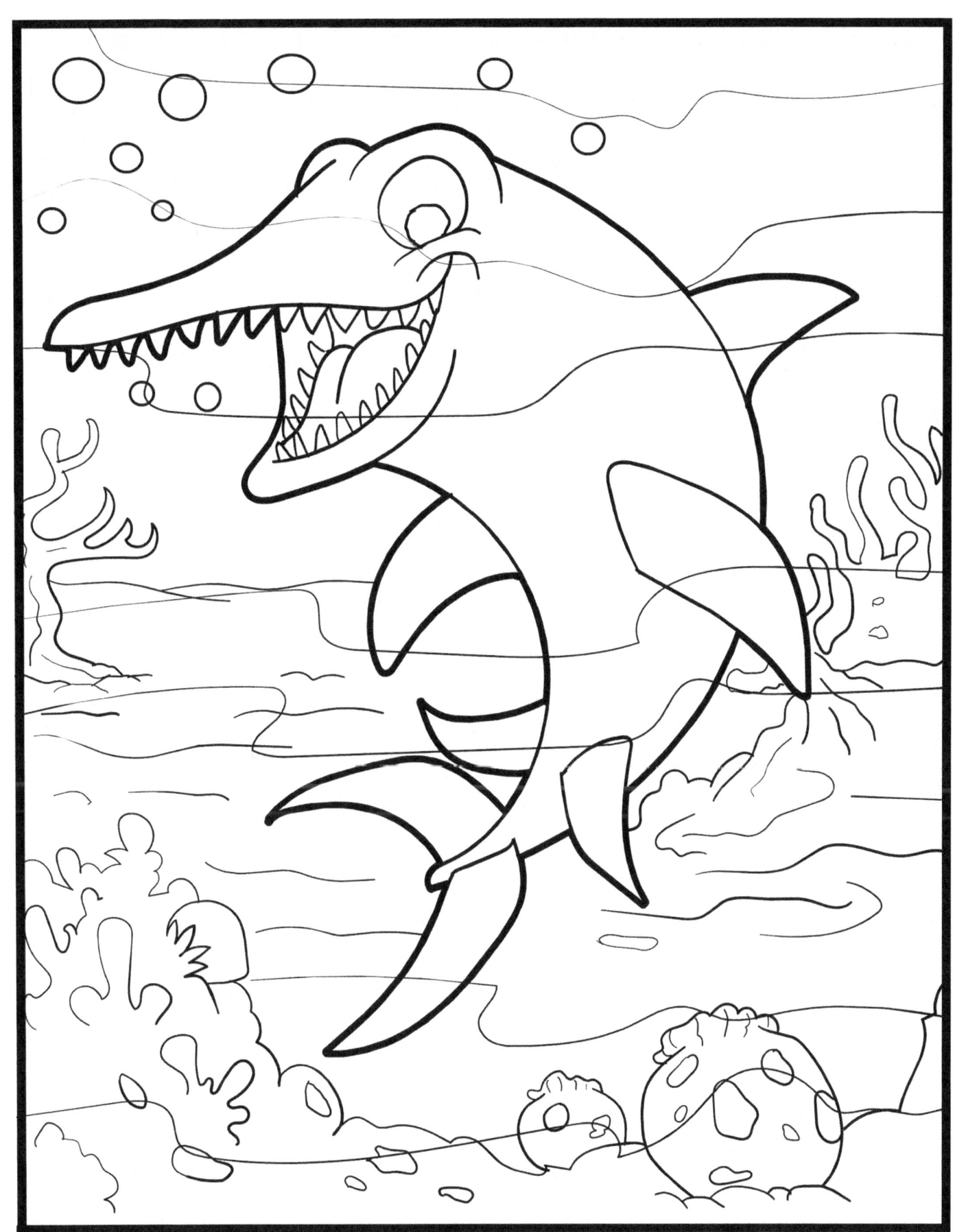

Ichthyosaurus

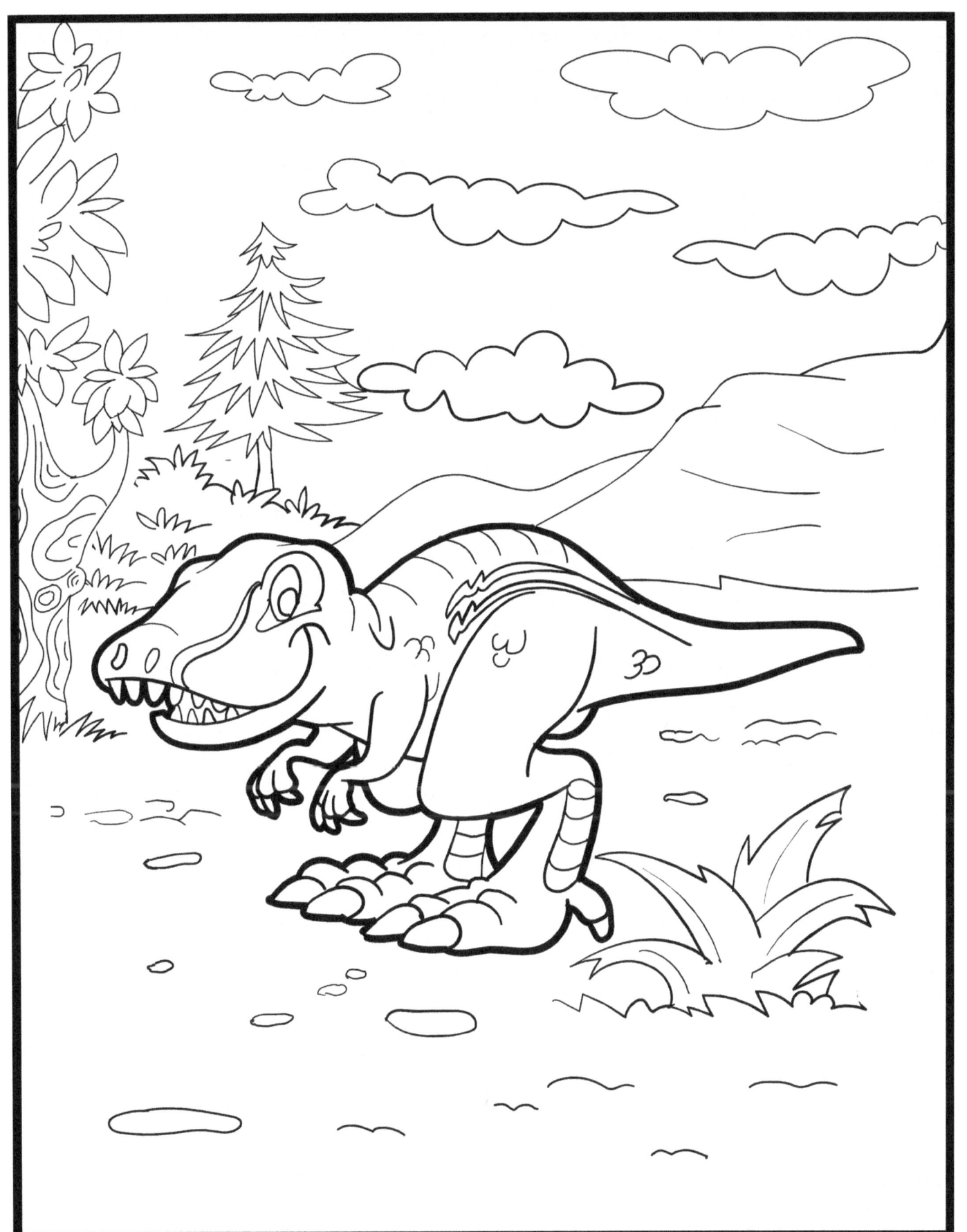

Iguanodon

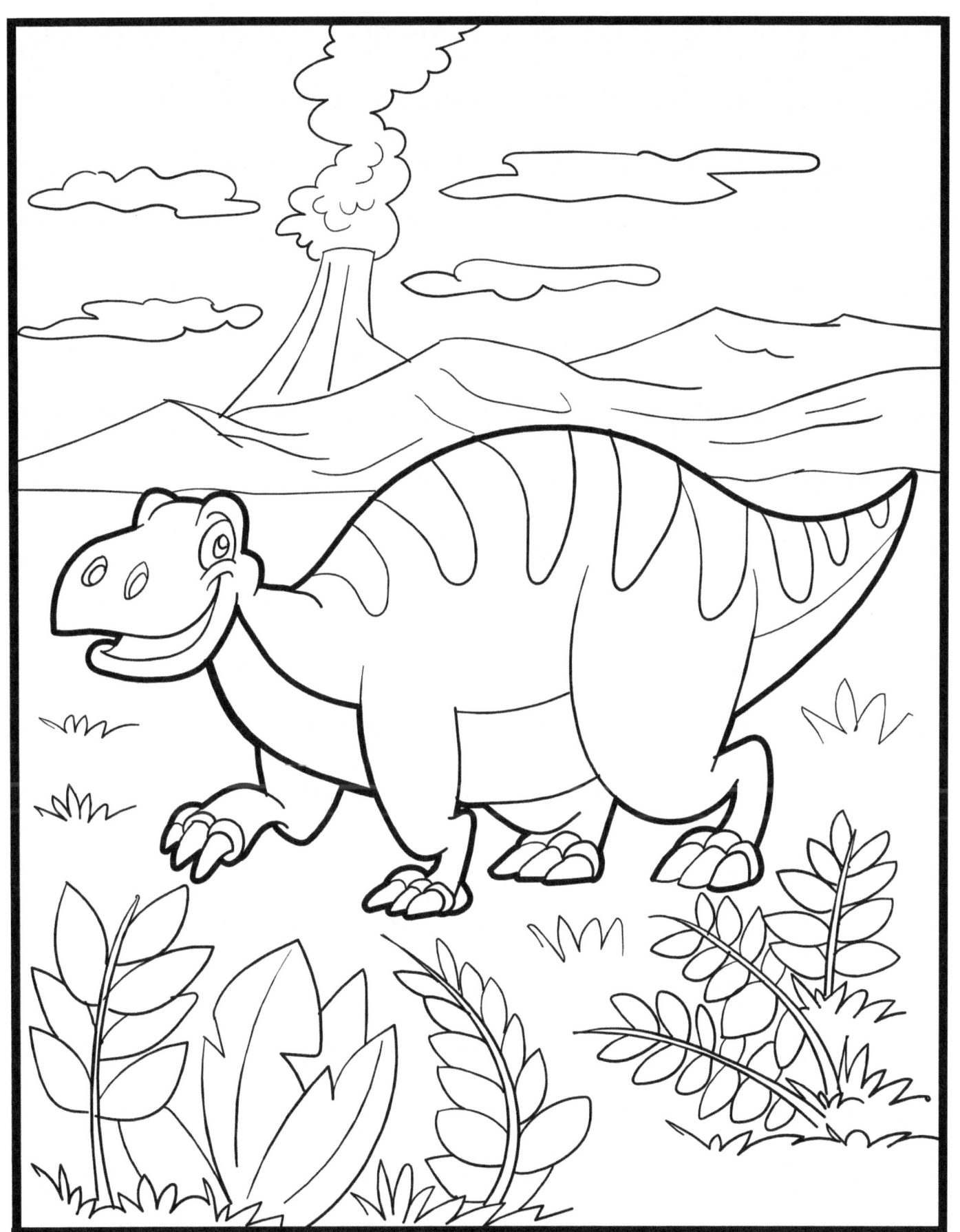

Isanosaurus

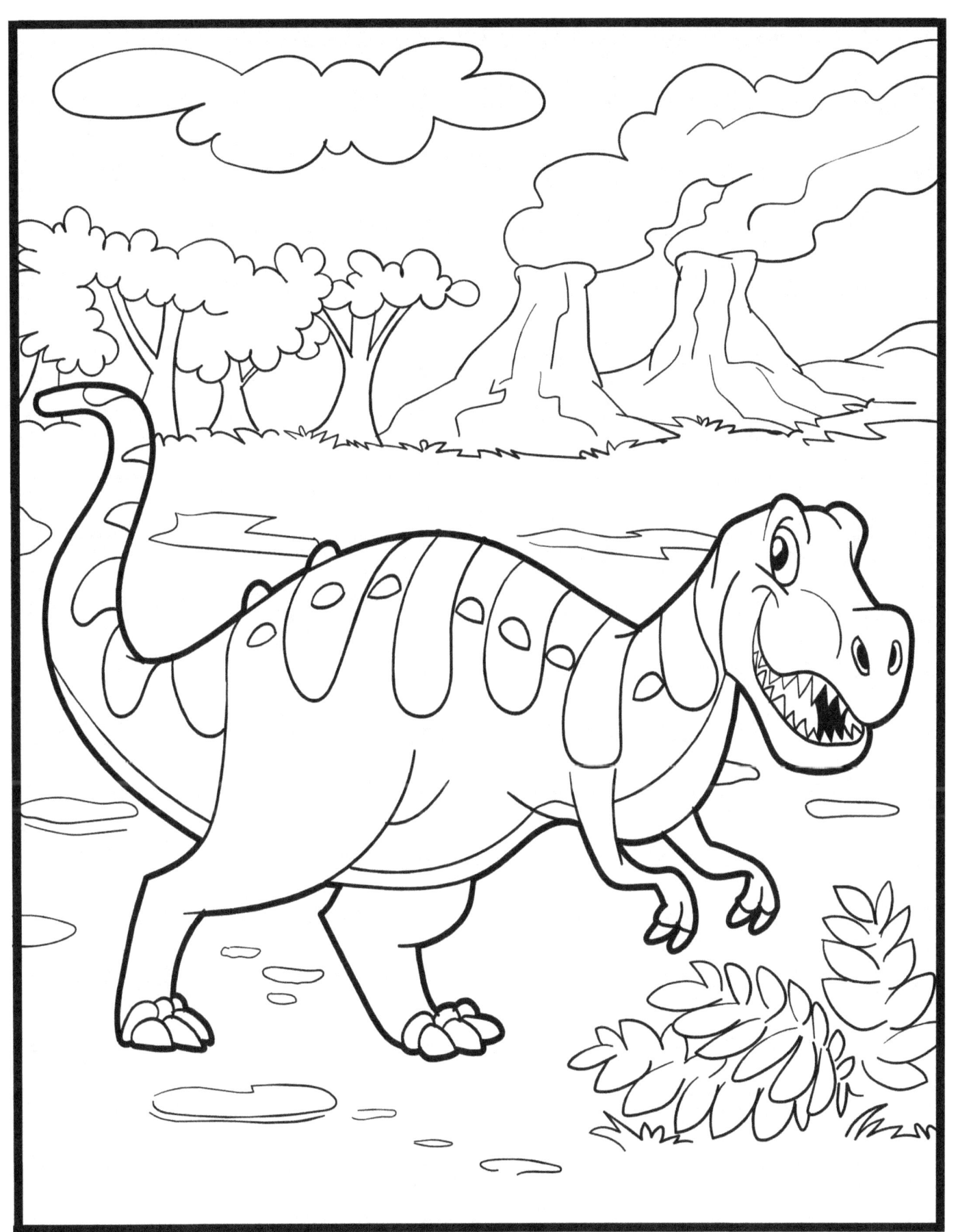

Majungasaurus

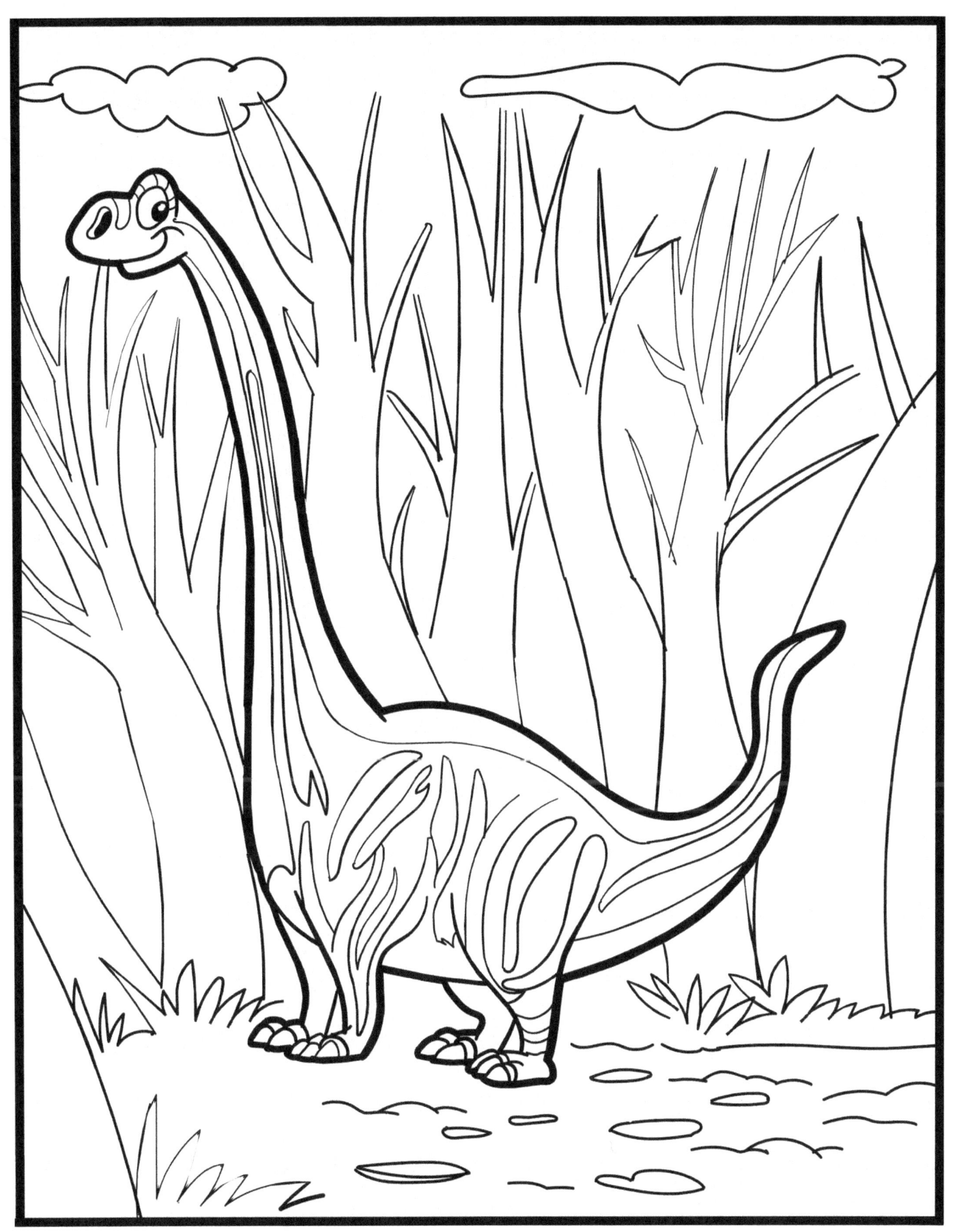

Mamenchisaurus

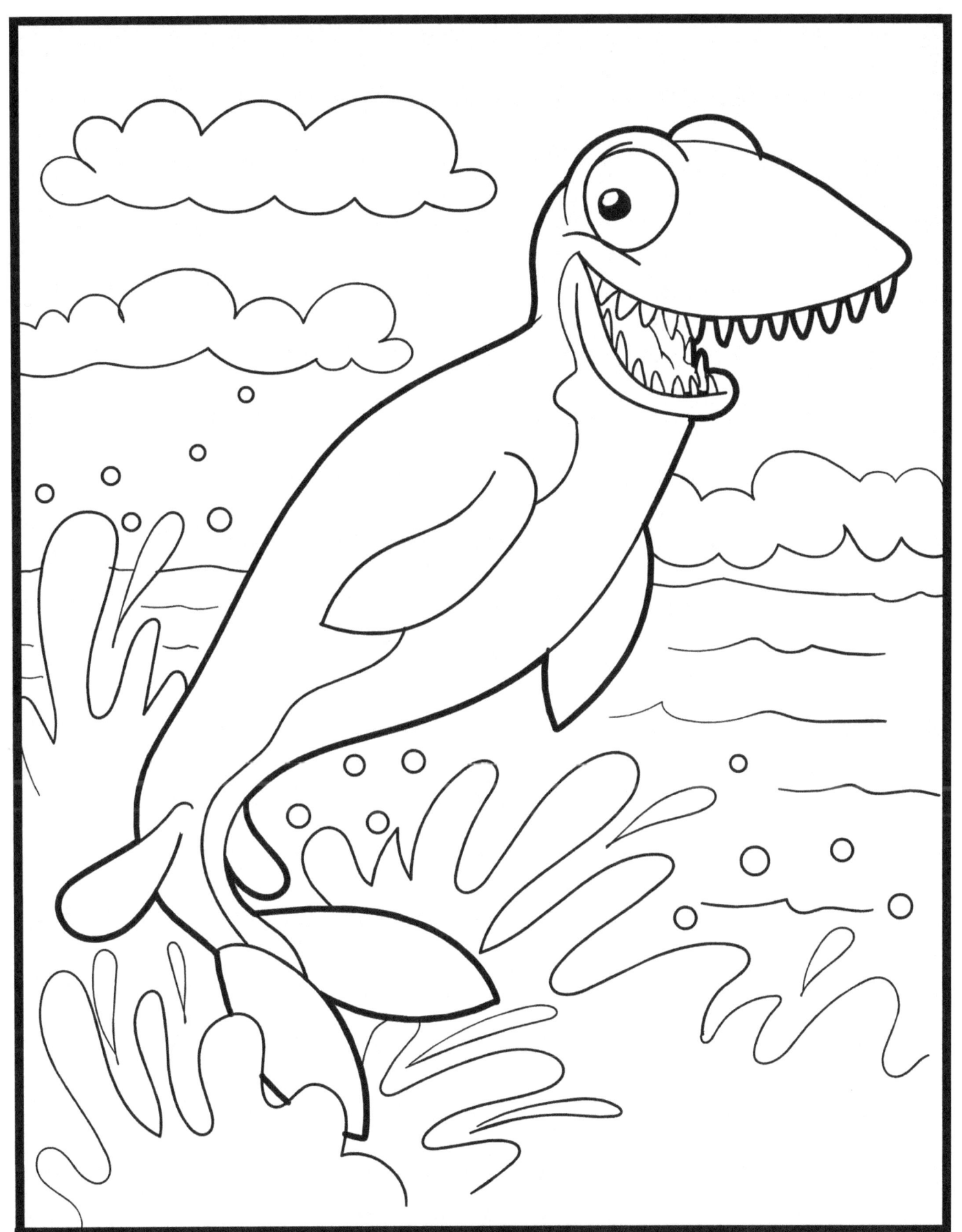

Mosasaurus

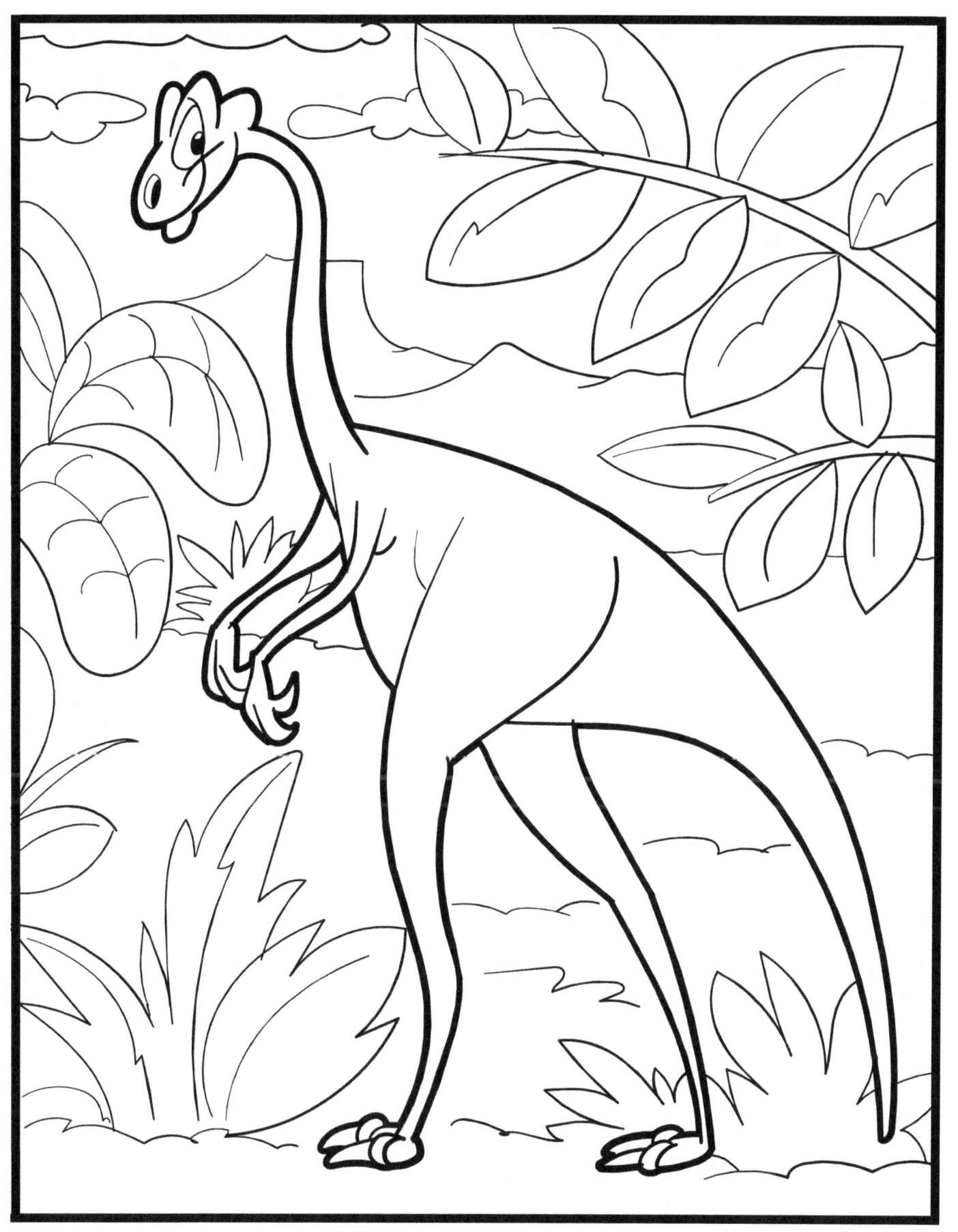

Ornithomimus

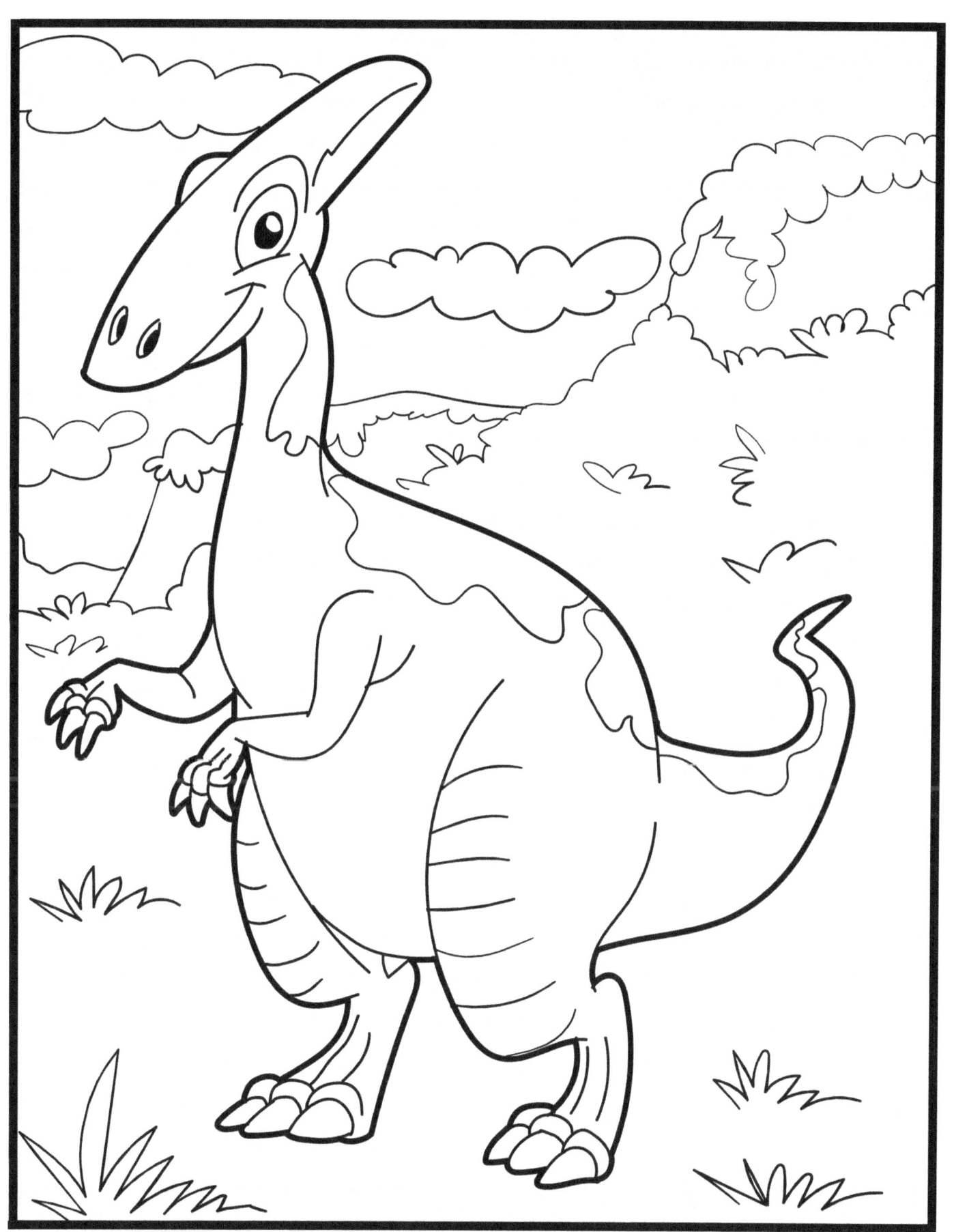

Parasaurolophus

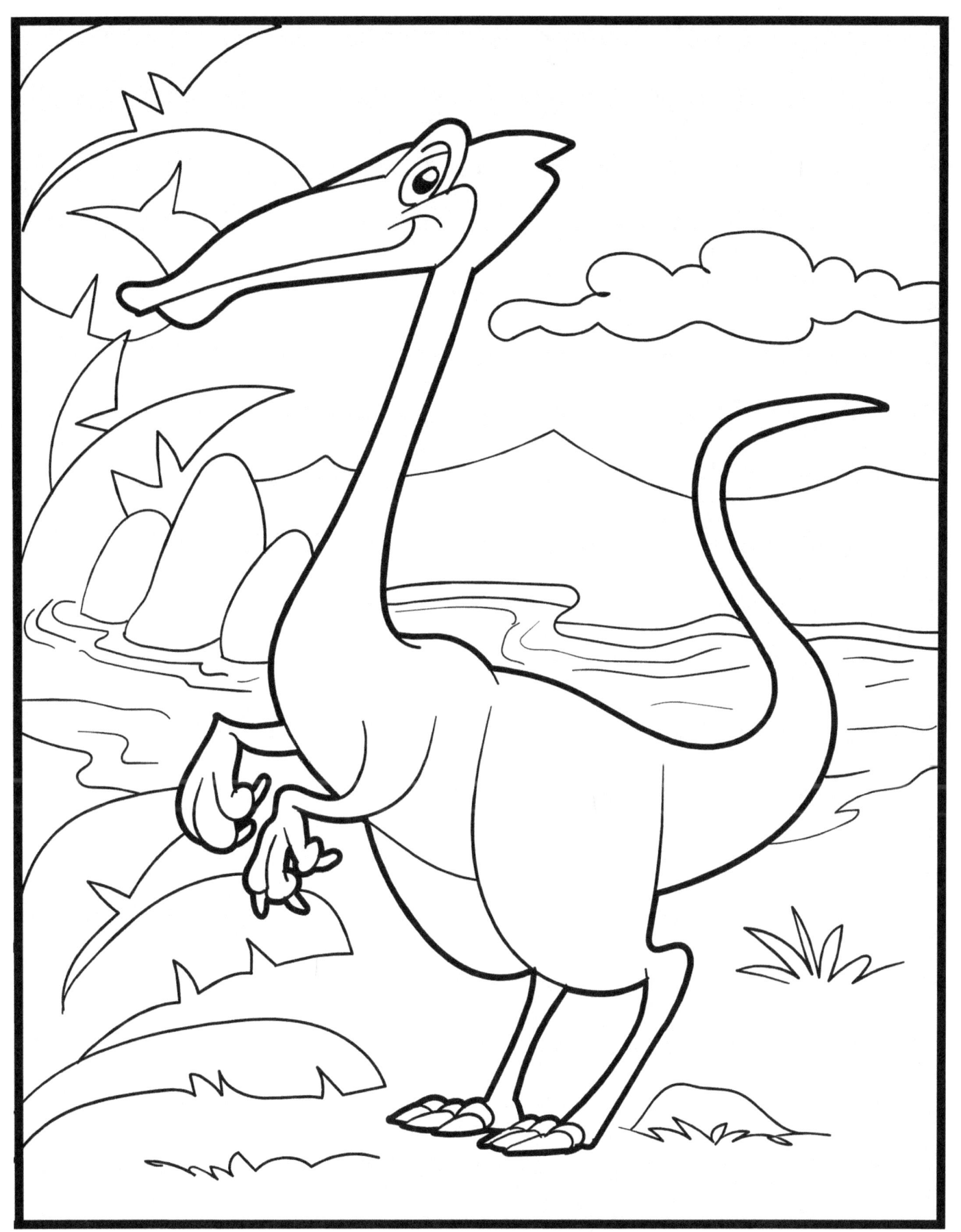

Pelicaninimus

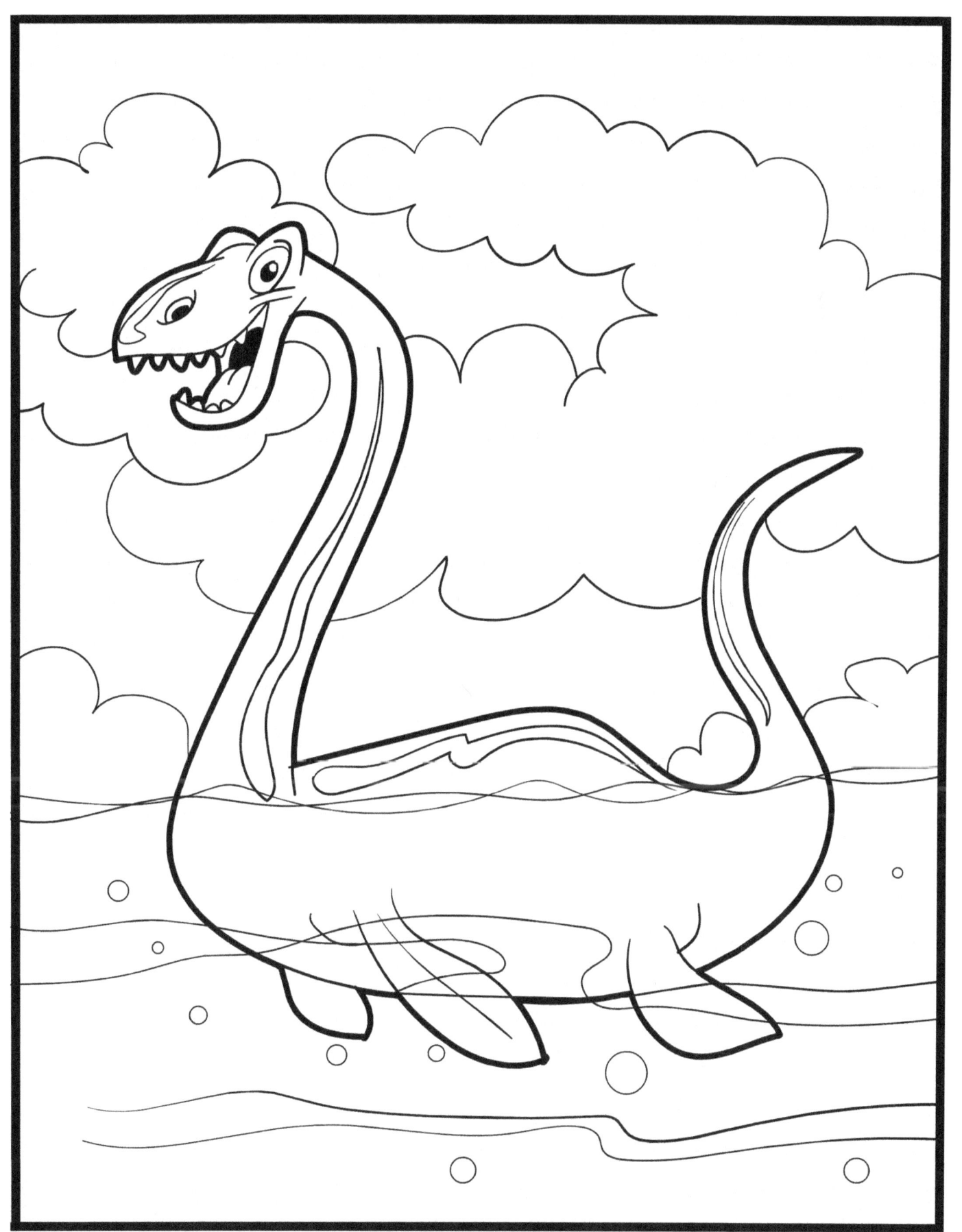

Plesiosaurier

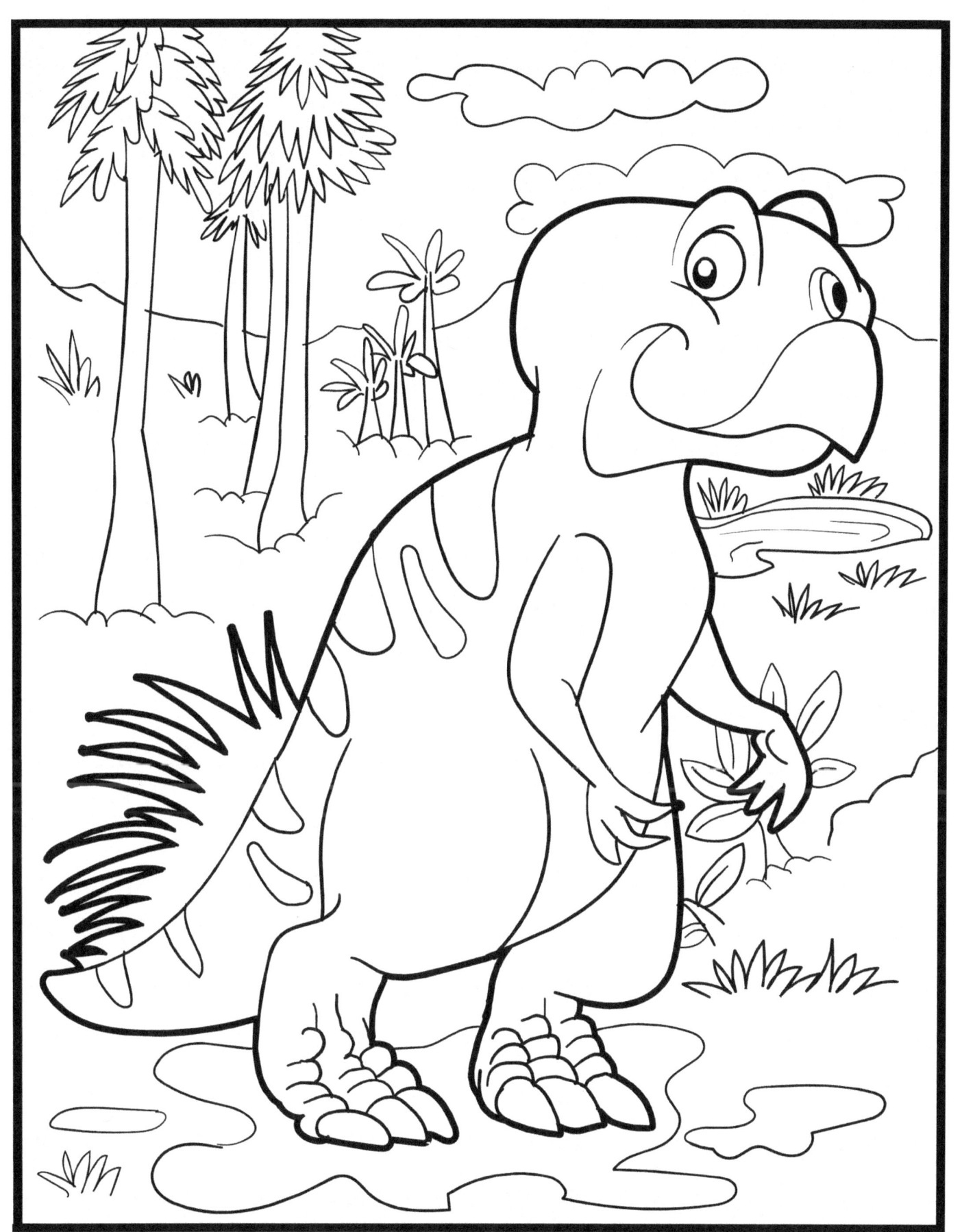

Psicattosaurus

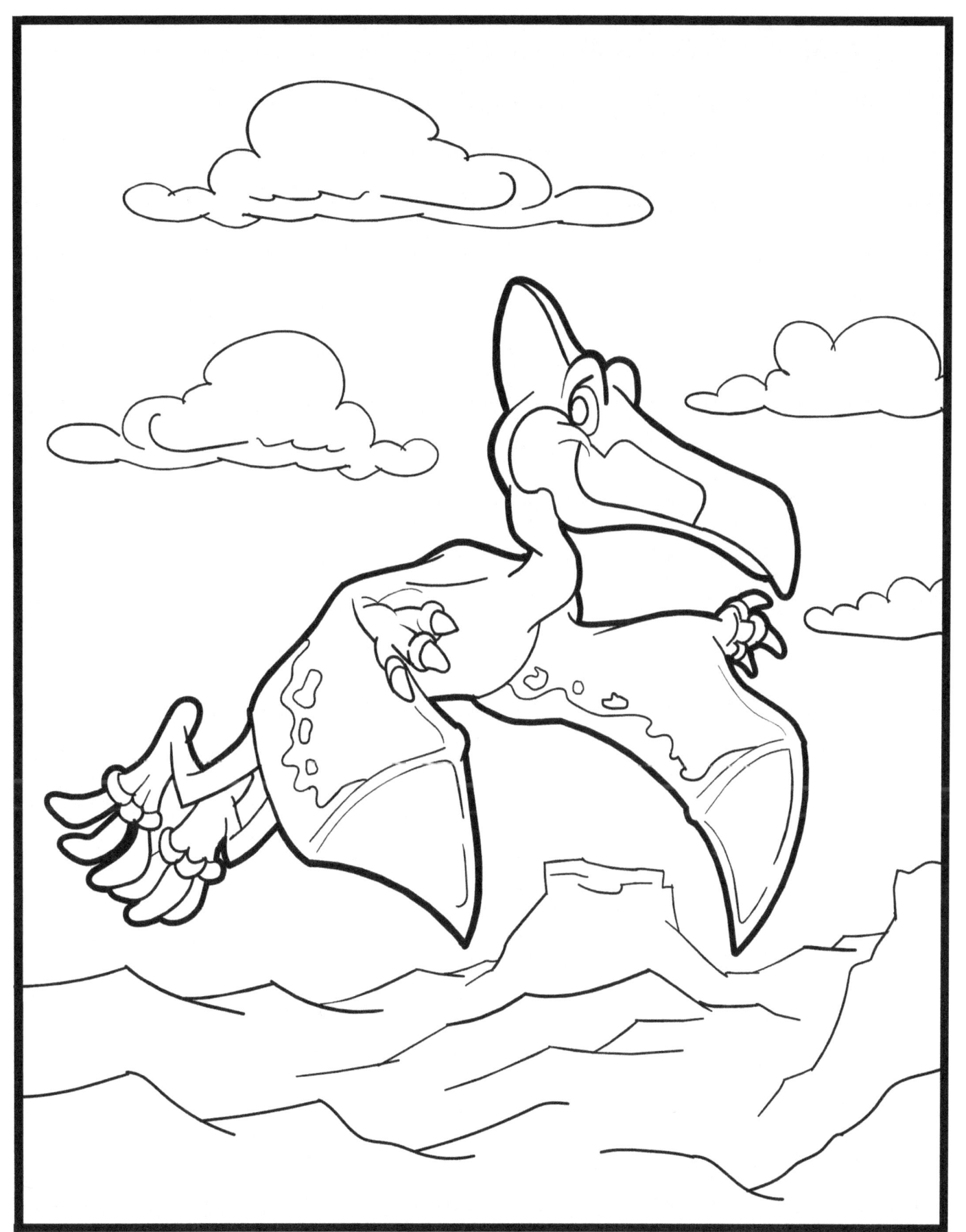

Pteranodon

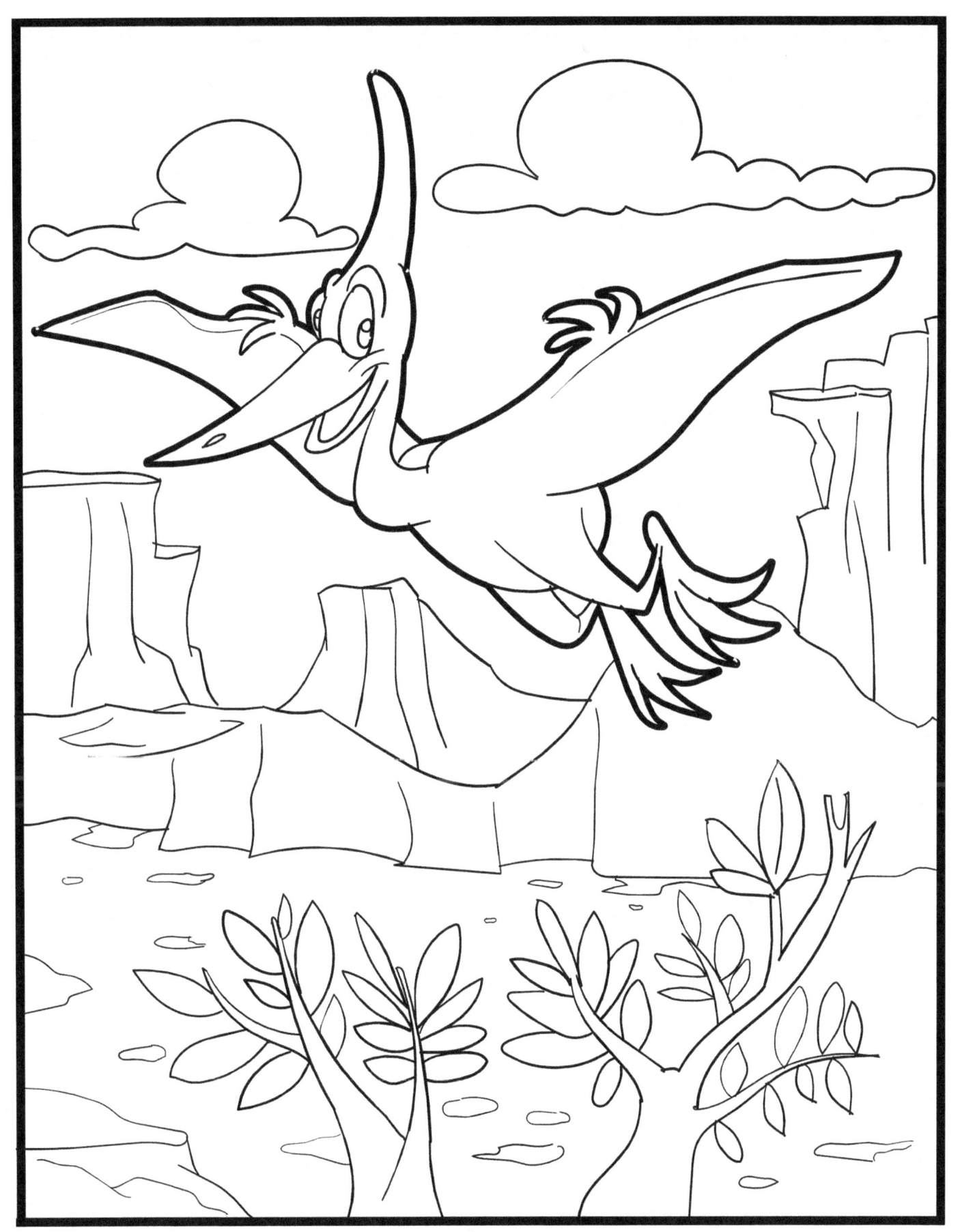

Pterodaktylus

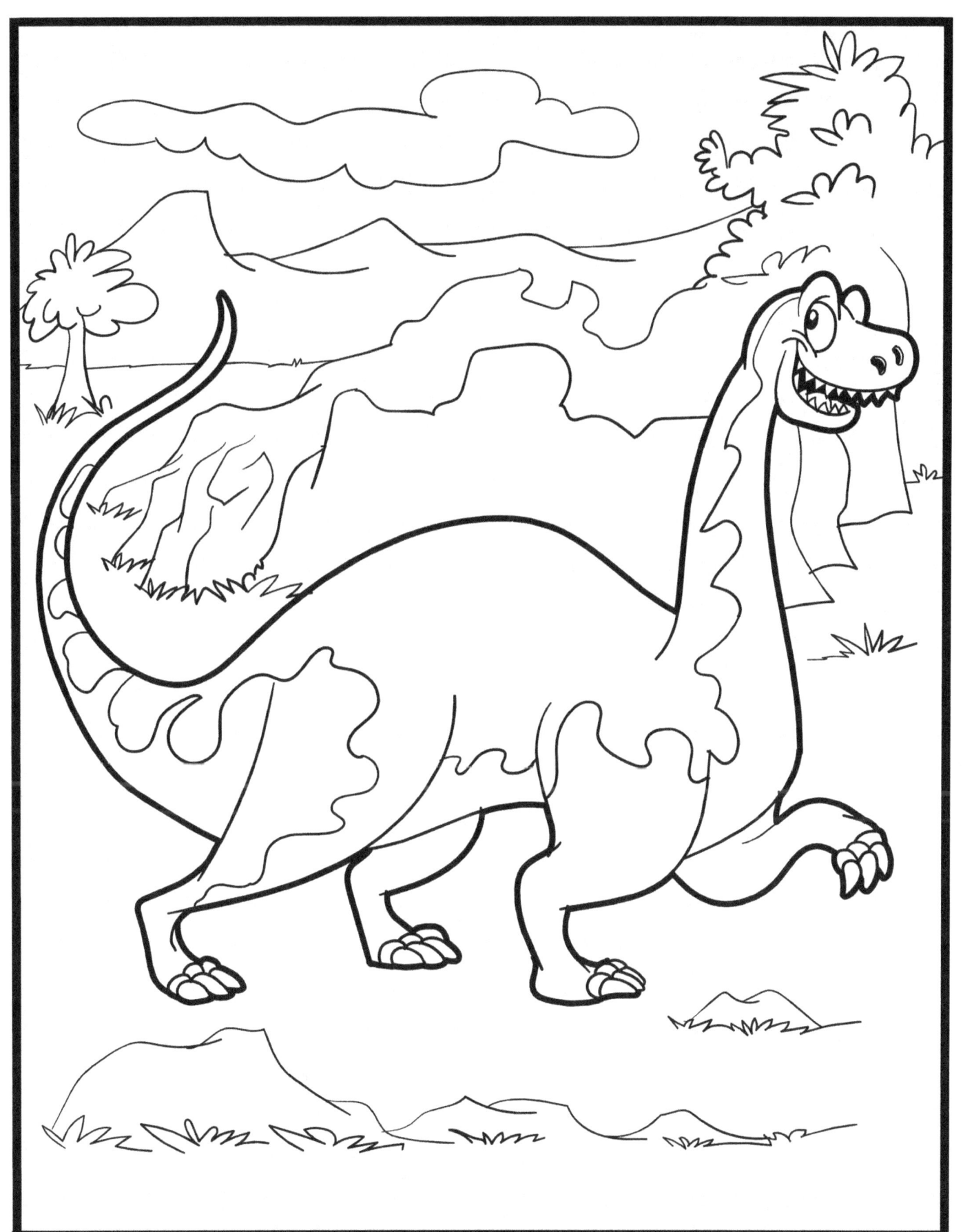

Riojasaurus

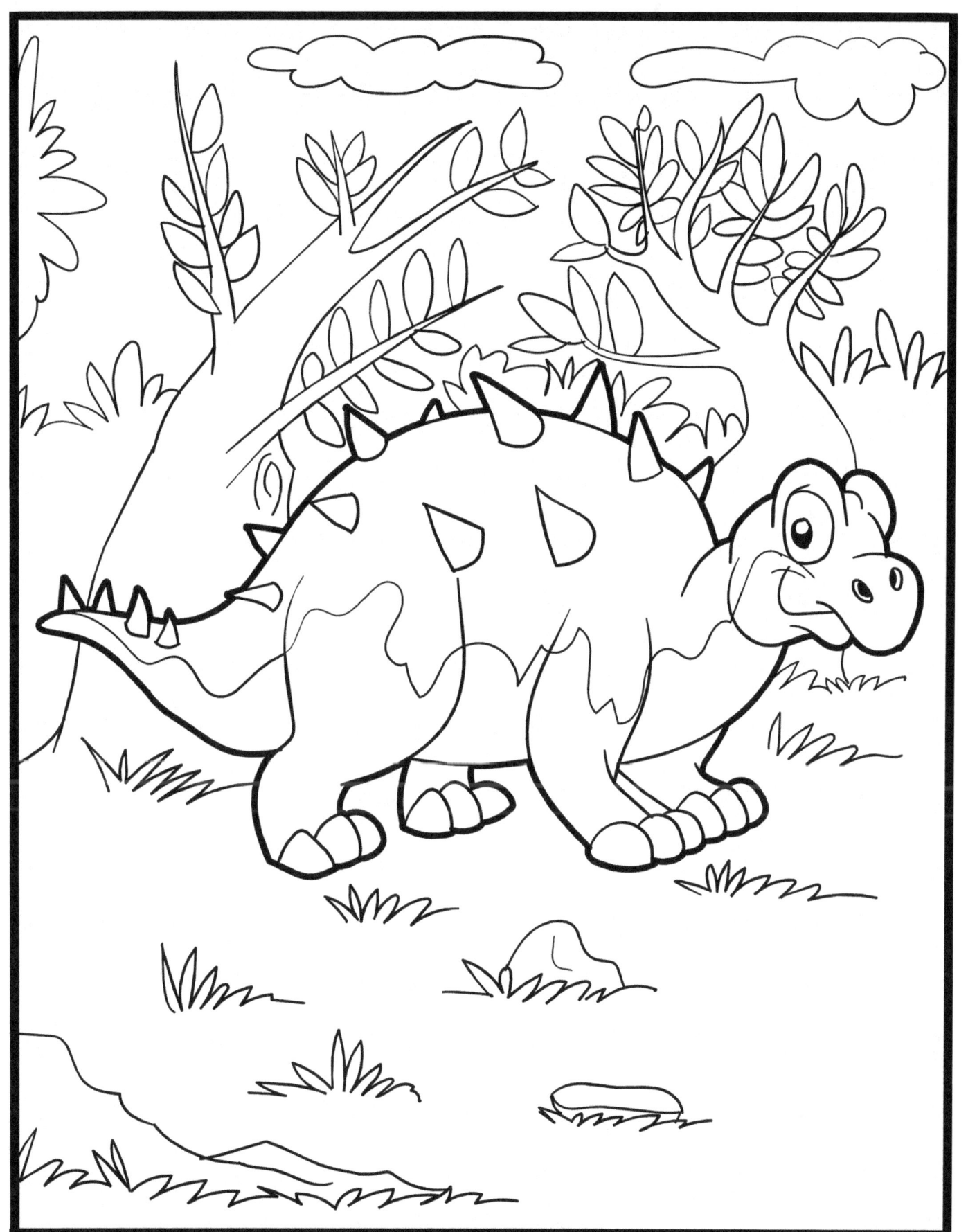

Silvisaurus

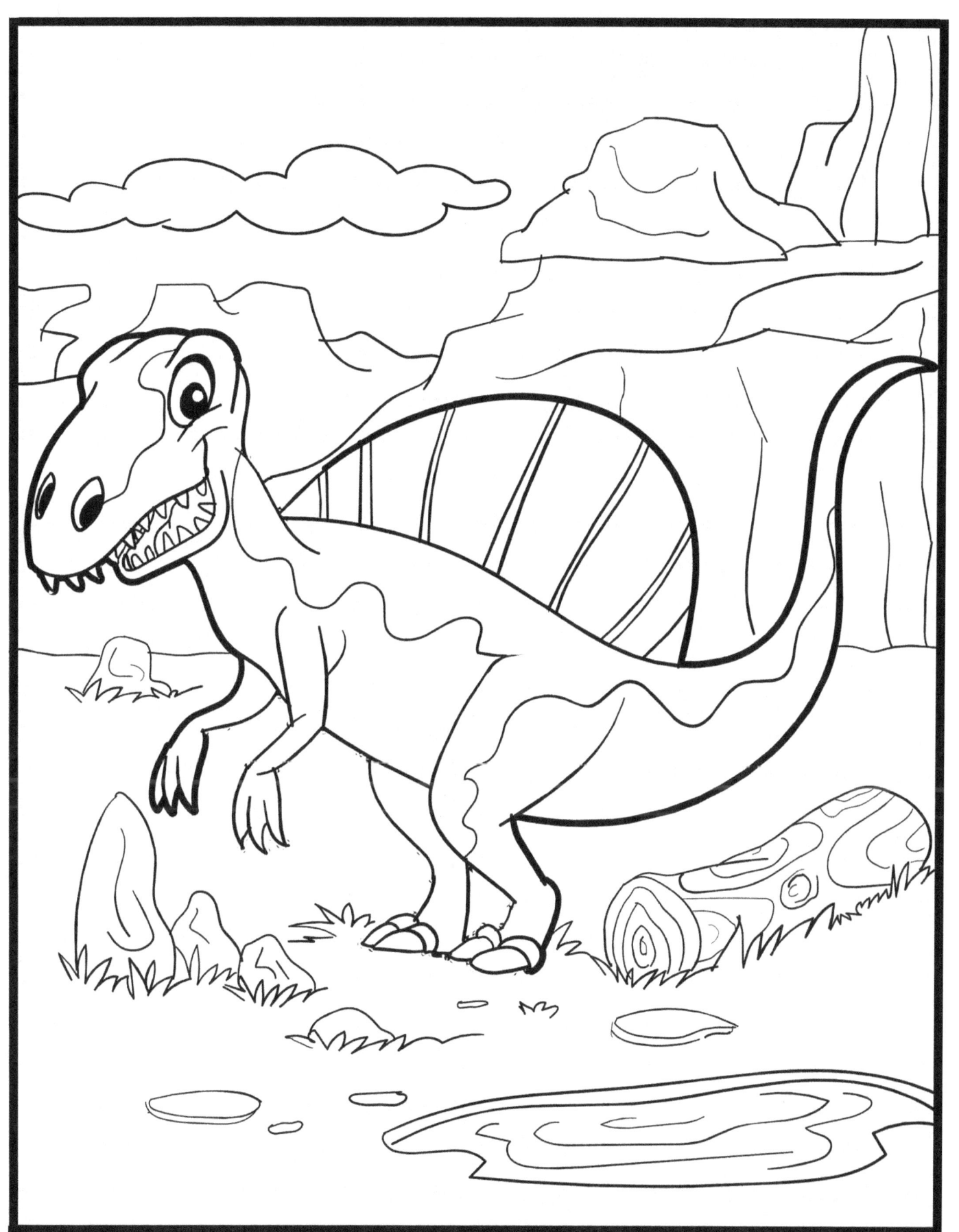

Spinosaurus

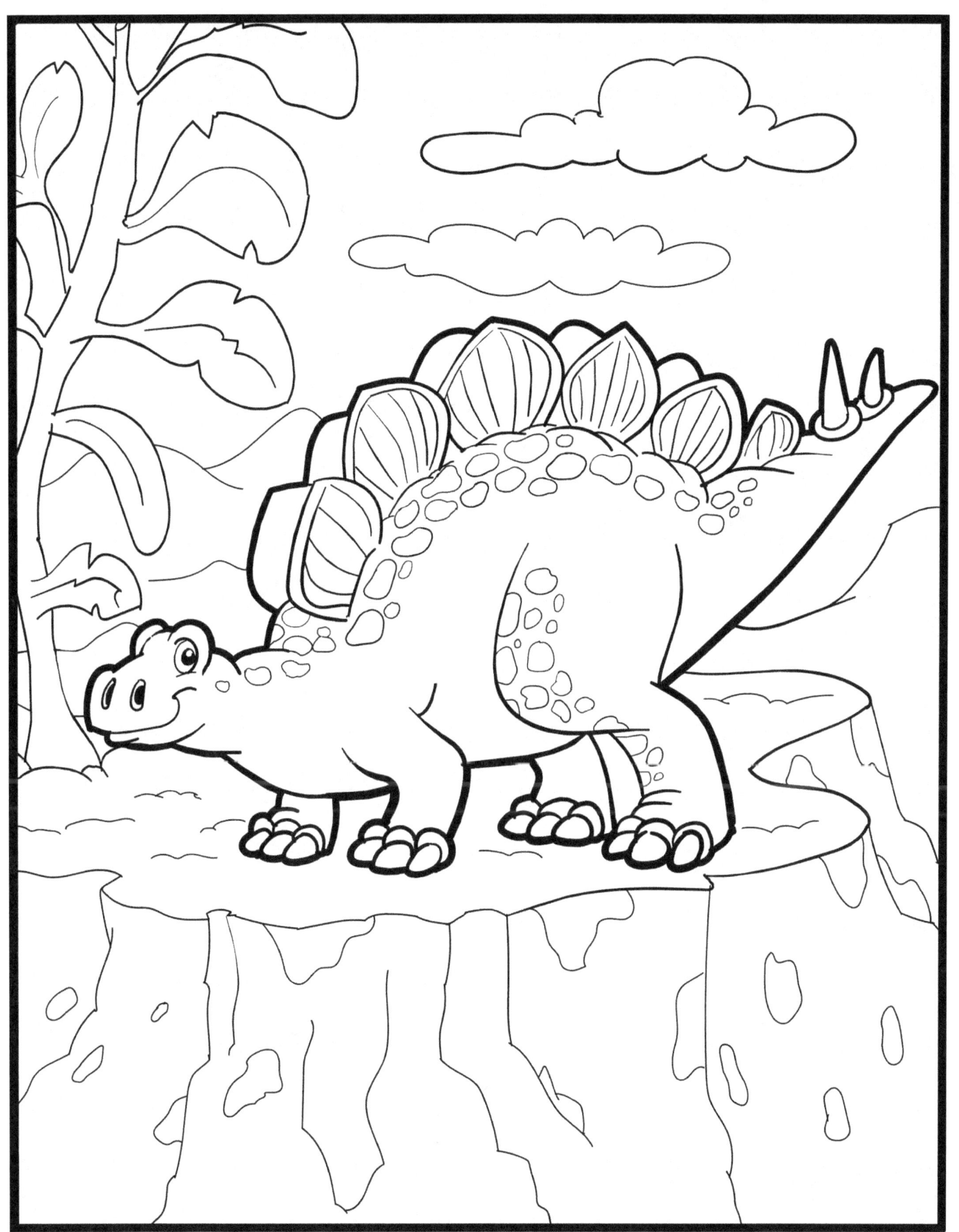

Stegosaurus

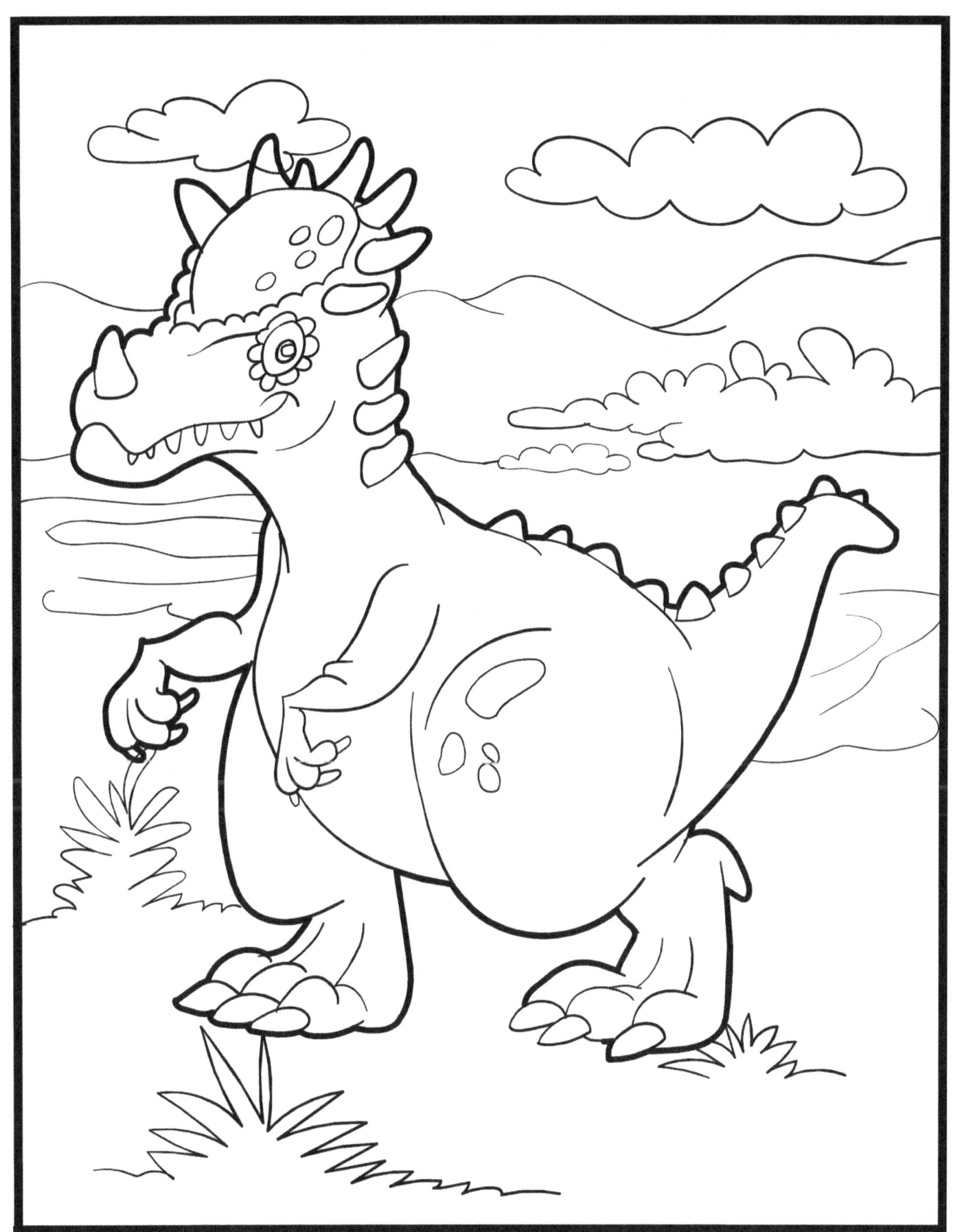

Stygimoloch

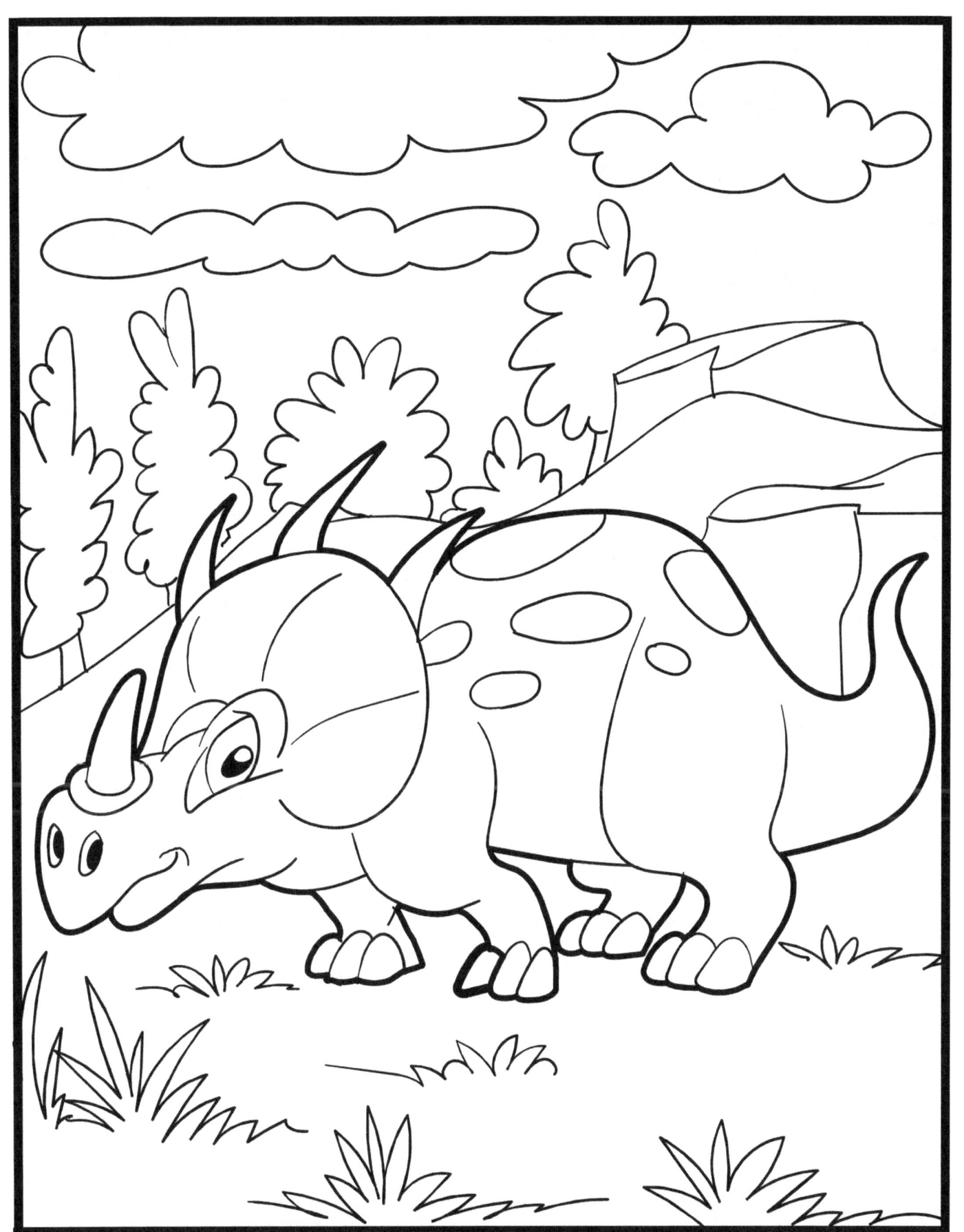

Styracosaurus

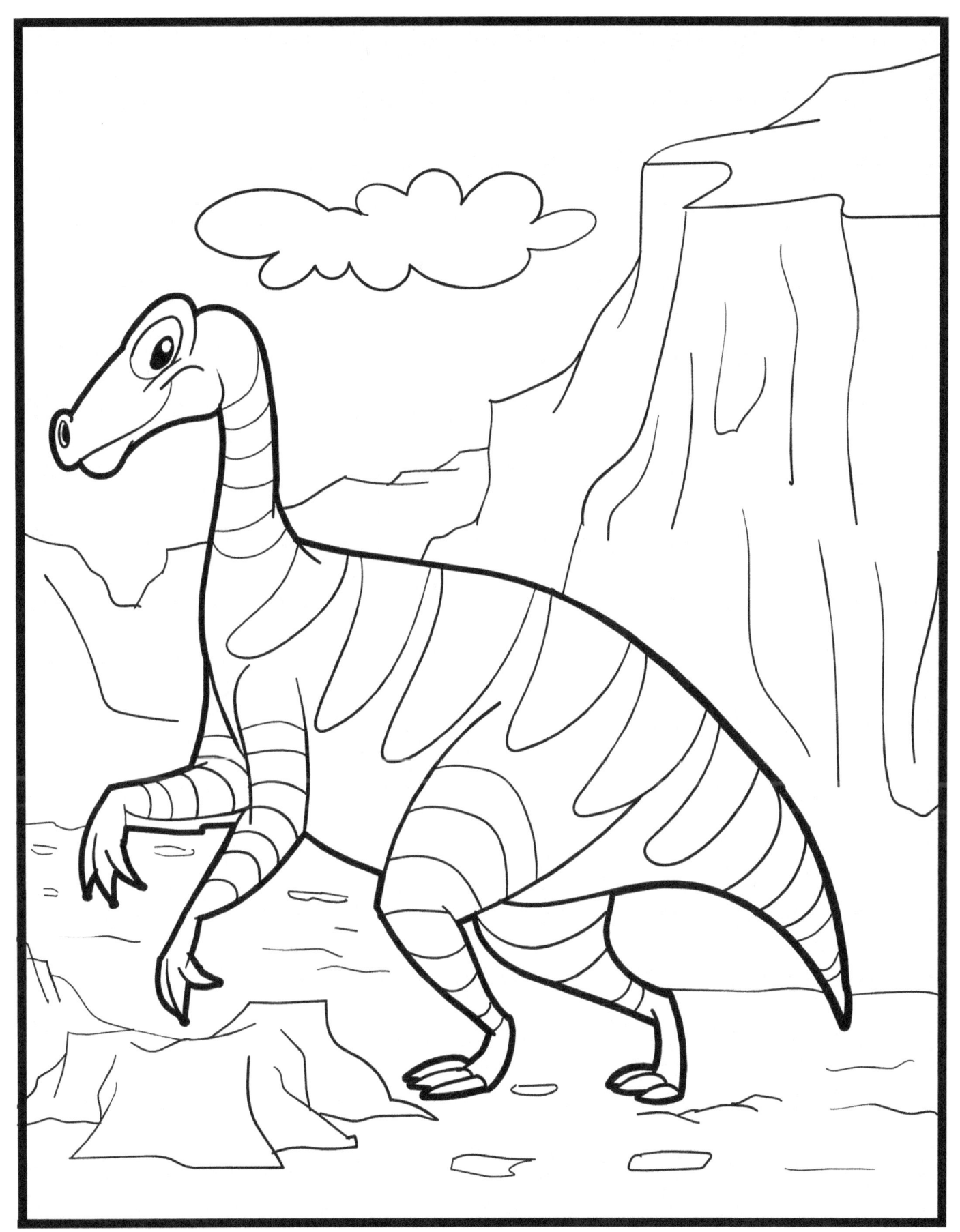

Decodontosaurus

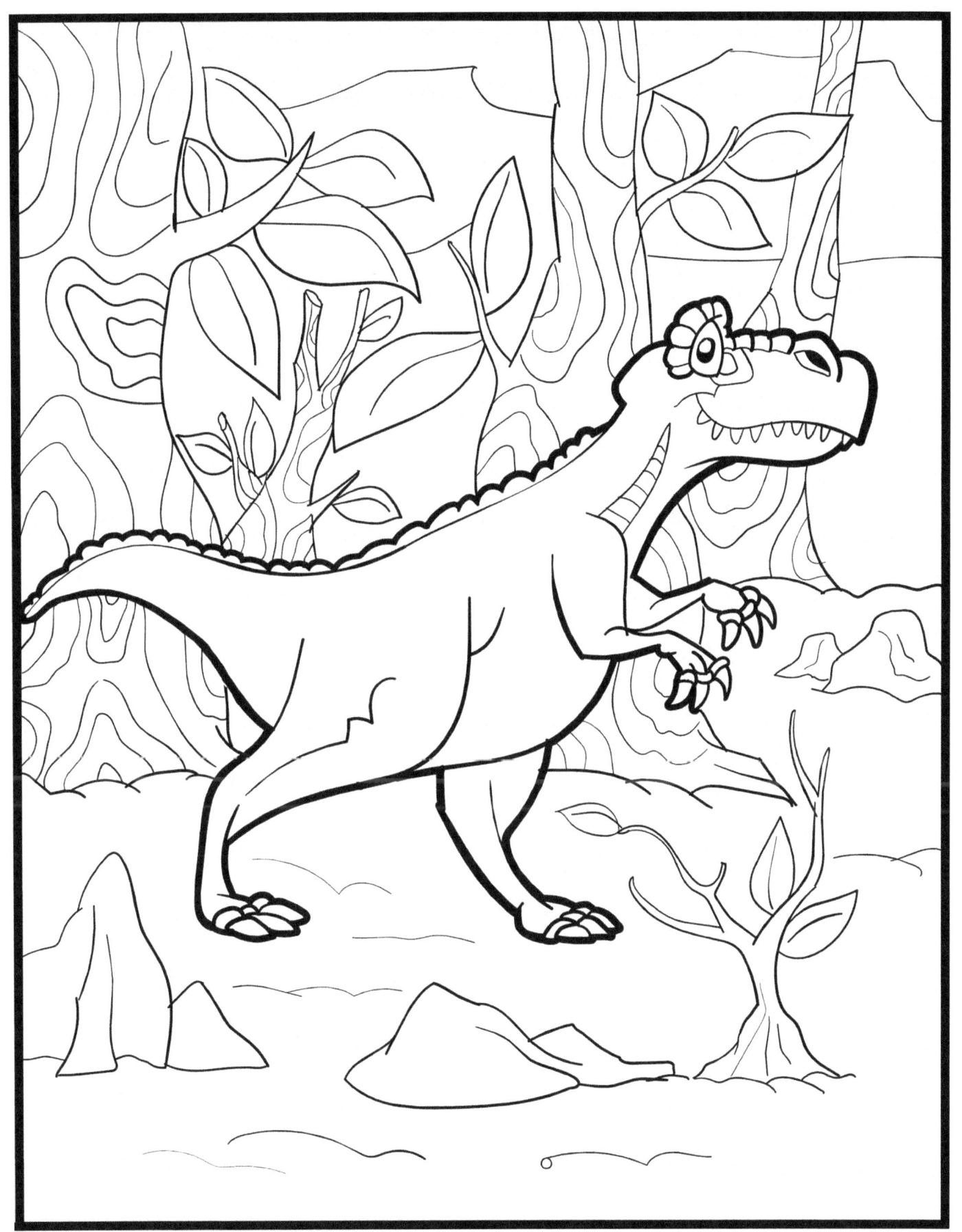

Tiranosaurus

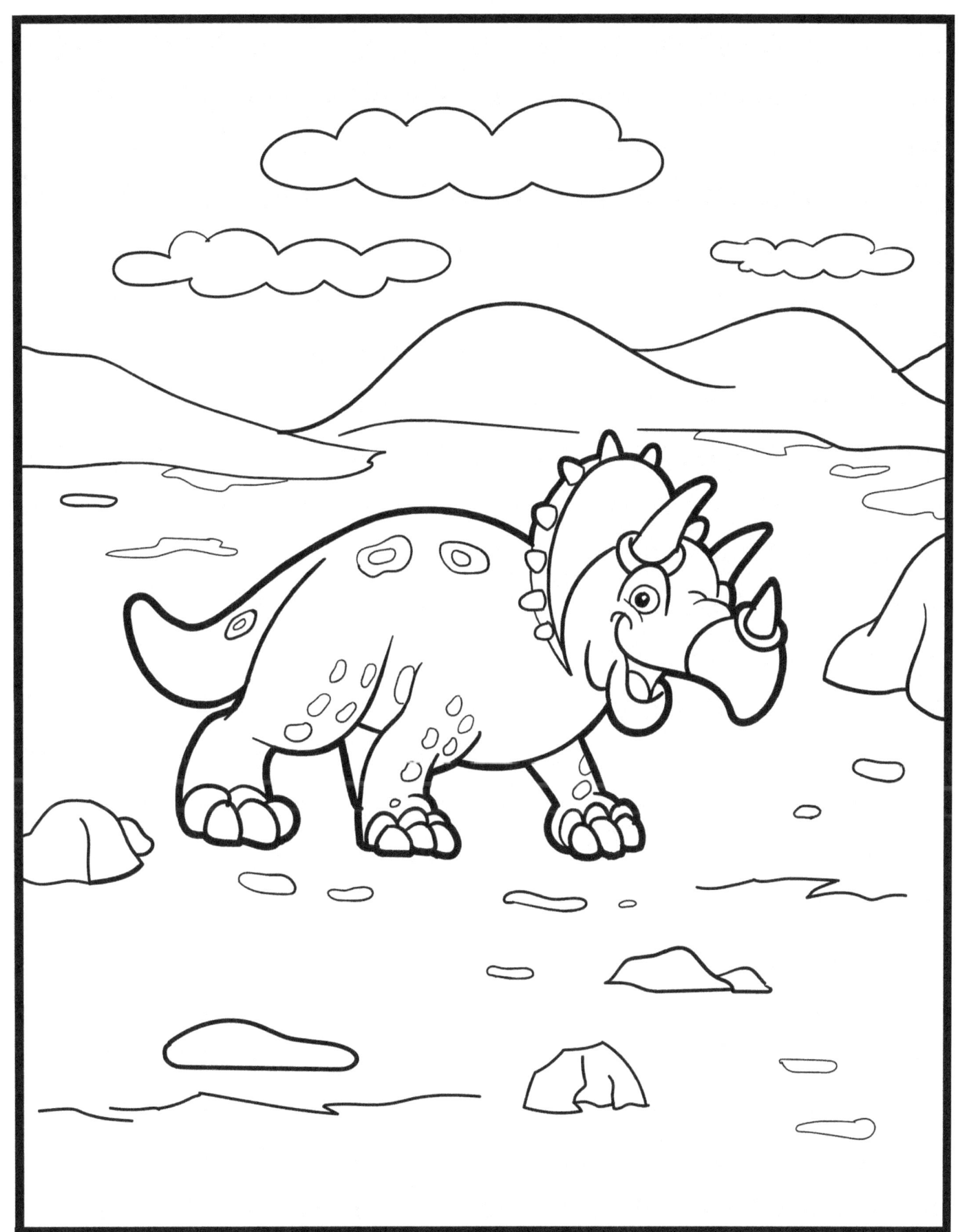

Triceratops

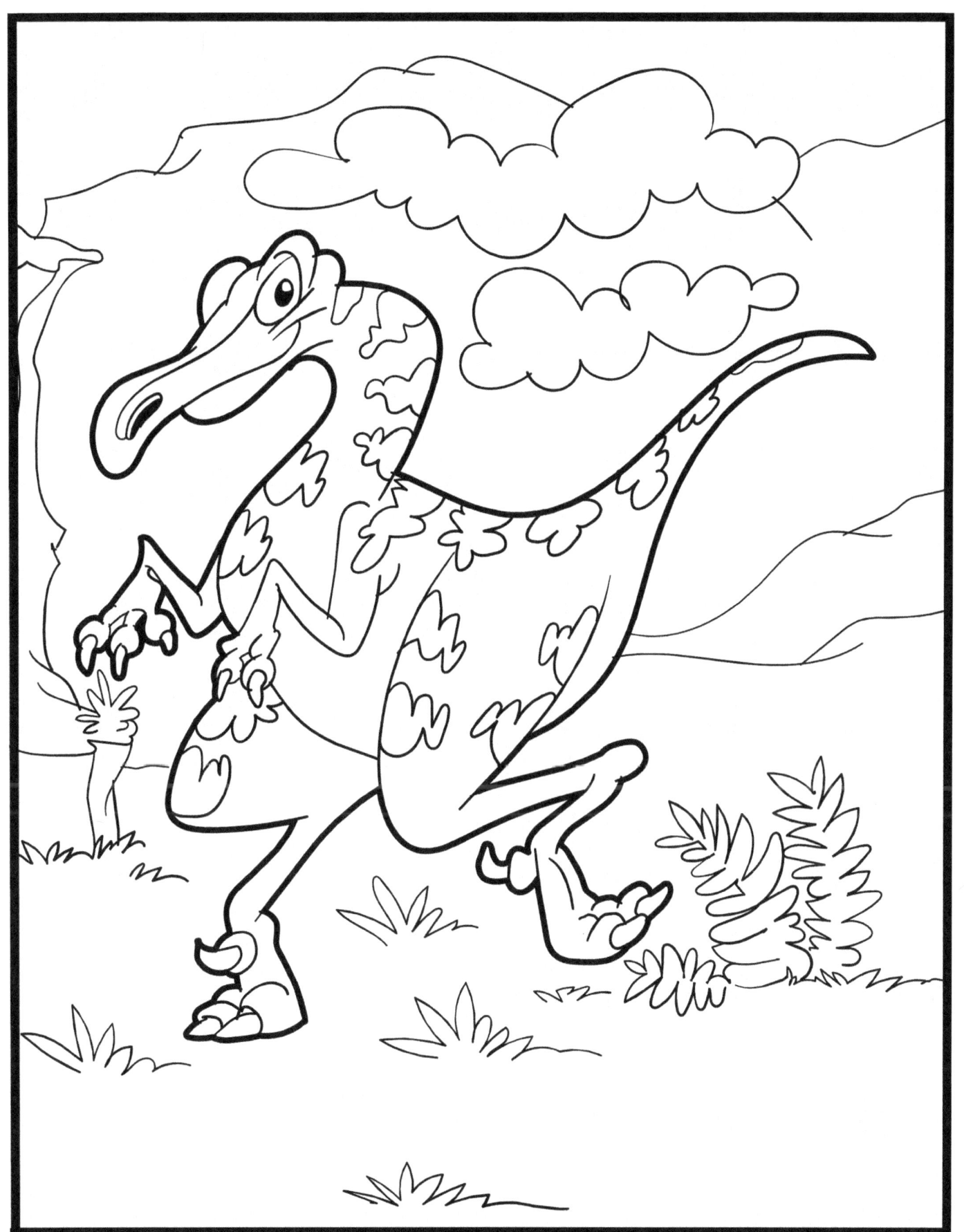

Troodon

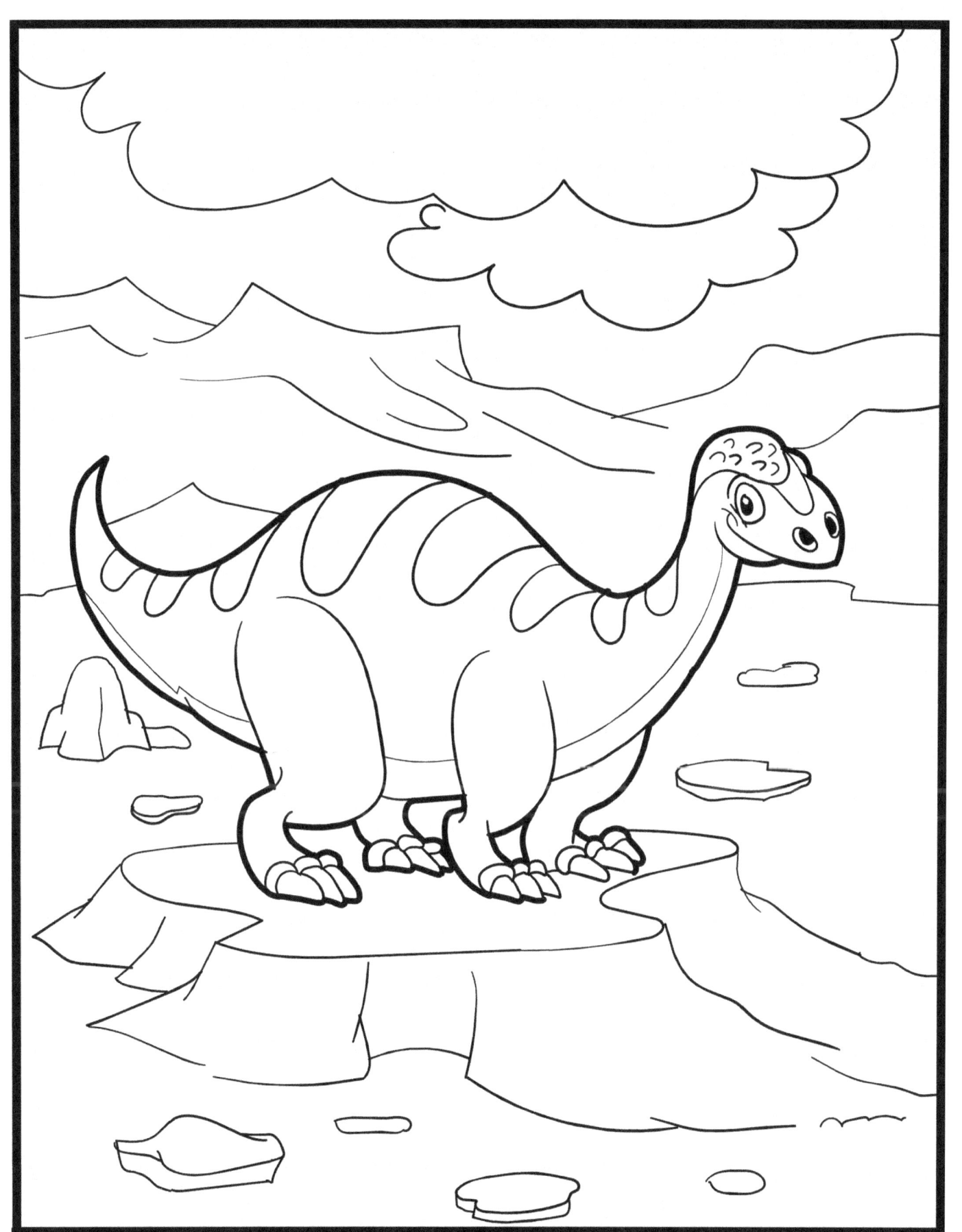

Tsintaosaurus

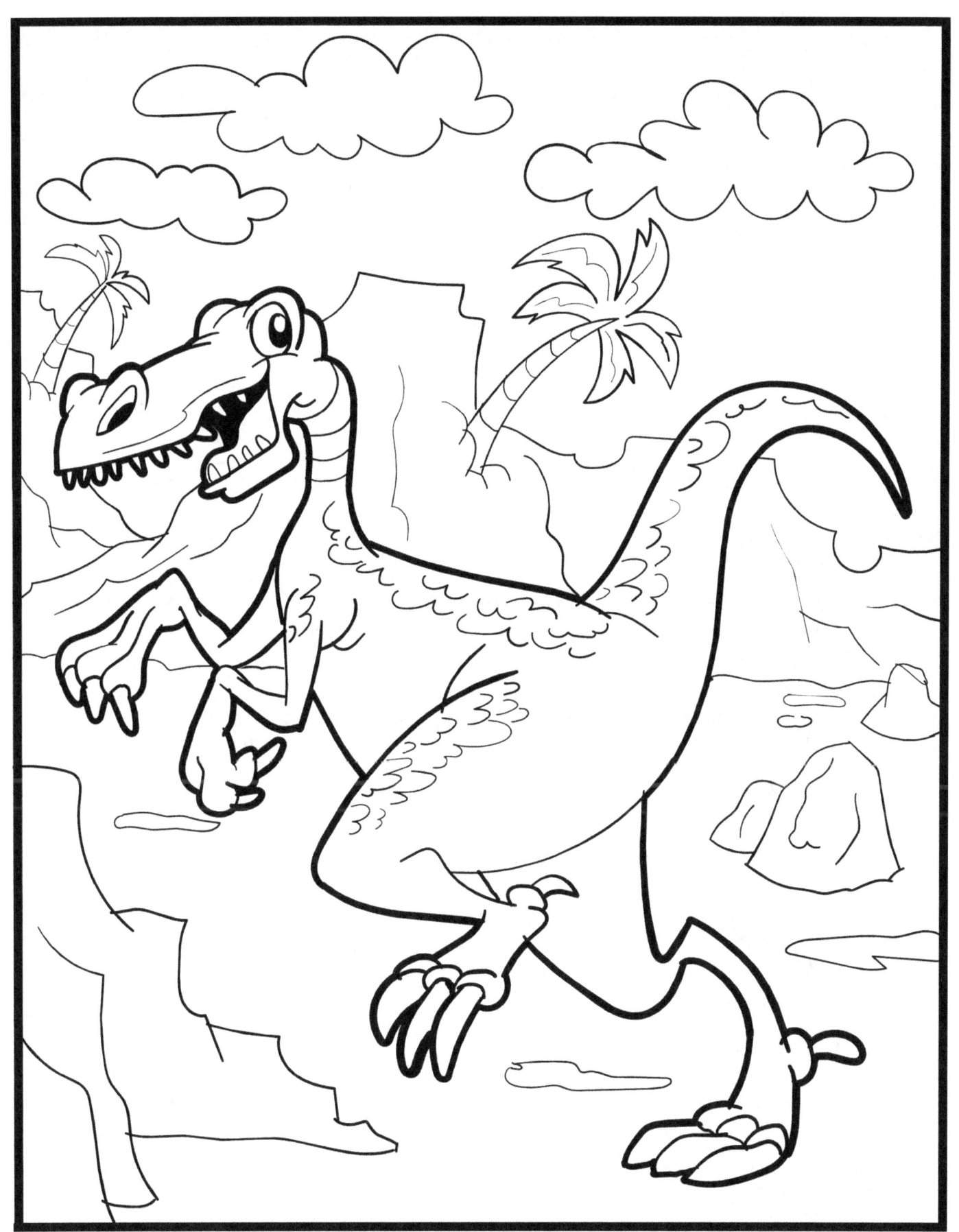

Velociraptor

Copyright

This publication, including its parts, is protected by copyright. Any commercial use is prohibited without the written consent of the publisher. This applies in particular to electronic or other duplication, translation, distribution, storage and public disclosure.

Dieses Werk, einschließlich seiner Teile, ist urheberrechtlich geschützt. Jede kommerzielle Verwertung ist ohne schriftliche Zustimmung des Herausgebers unzulässig. Dies gilt insbesondere für die elektronische oder sonstige Vervielfältigung, Übersetzung, Verbreitung, Speicherung und öffentliche Zugänglichmachung.

Imprint / Impressum

Digital Front GmbH
Mergenthalerallee 73-75
65760 Eschborn
Deutschland (Germany)

E-Mail: info@digital-front.de

Representatives / Vertretungsberechtigte:
Alexander Mendelson, Leonid Ravin

Address / Anschrift:
Mergenthalerallee 73-75
65760 Eschborn
Deutschland (Germany)

www.ingramcontent.com/pod-product-compliance
Lightning Source LLC
Chambersburg PA
CBHW081443220526
45466CB00008B/2492